# America's Rome

## ARTISTS IN THE ETERNAL CITY, 1800–1900

BY WILLIAM L. VANCE,

MARY K. McGUIGAN, AND

JOHN F. McGUIGAN JR.

EDITOR
PAUL S. D'AMBROSIO

Fenimore Art Museum
Lake Road — Cooperstown, New York
www.fenimoreartmuseum.org

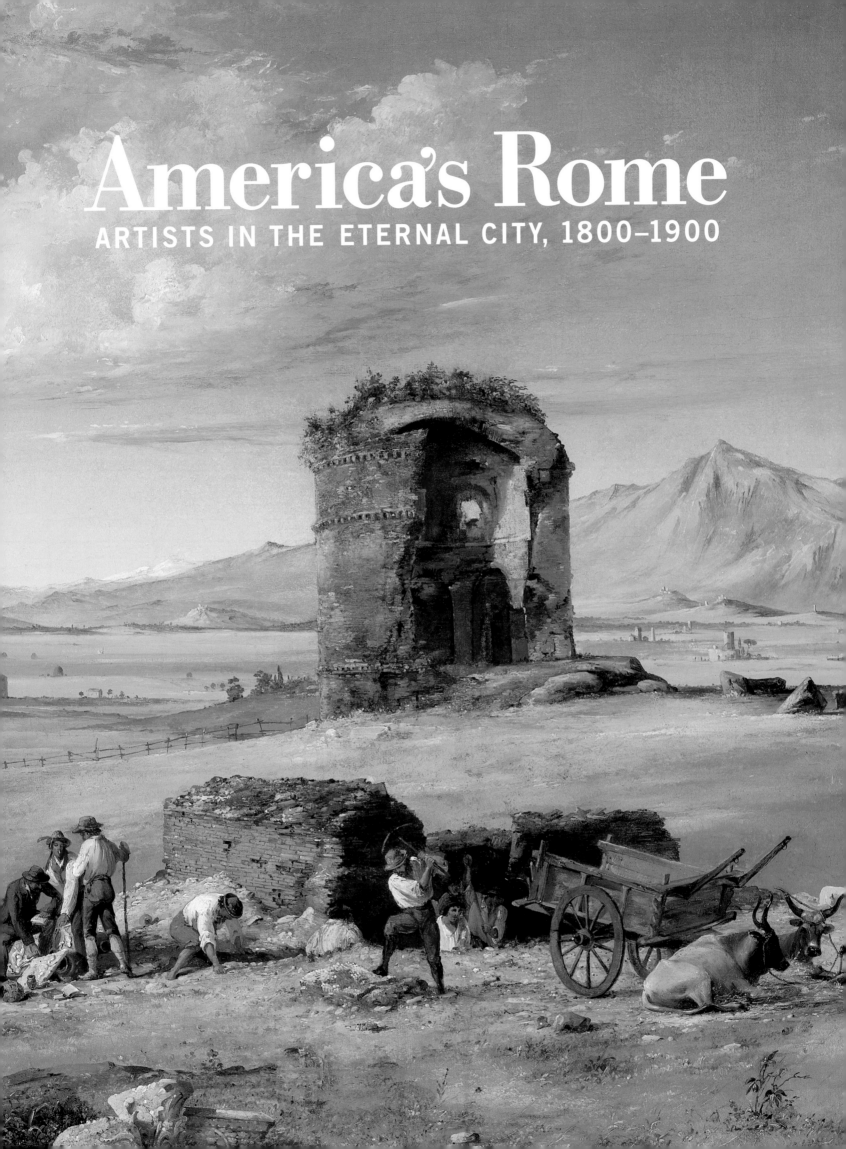

# America's Rome

## ARTISTS IN THE ETERNAL CITY, 1800–1900

# America's Rome

## ARTISTS IN THE ETERNAL CITY, 1800–1900

BY WILLIAM L. VANCE,
MARY K. McGUIGAN, AND
JOHN F. McGUIGAN JR.

EDITOR: PAUL S. D'AMBROSIO
DESIGN: RICHARD P. NADEAU

First published in 2009 by the Fenimore Art Museum
Lake Road – P.O. Box 800 • Cooperstown, NY 13326
www.fenimoreartmuseum.org

Published in conjunction with the exhibition *America's Rome:
Artists in the Eternal City, 1800–1900*, on view at the Fenimore Art
Museum, Cooperstown, N.Y., May 23–December 31, 2009

This exhibition and catalogue are made possible through the generous
contributions of the Tianaderrah Foundation, the International Music
and Art Foundation, the Dixon Ryan Fox Fund of the New York State
Historical Association, and the patronage of Comm. Stefano E. D. Acunto,
Hon. Vice Consul, Republic of Italy.

Production: Nadeau Design Associates, Utica, N.Y.
Printing: Brodock Press, Utica, N.Y.
Principal Photography: John Bigelow Taylor
Exhibition Management and Design: Michelle Murdock,
Christine Rossi, Nisha Bansil, and Christine Olsen

ISBN: 978-0-917334-36-1

# Contents

Foreword
Paul S. D'Ambrosio                                    7

America's Rome
William L. Vance                                      9

"This Market of Physiognomy"
American Artists and Rome's Art Academies,
Life Schools, and Models, 1825–1870
Mary K. McGuigan                                     39

American Open-Air Landscape
Painting in Rome, 1825–1885
John F. McGuigan Jr.                                 73

Selected Bibliography                               120

Lenders to the Exhibition                           122

6

# Foreword

PAUL S. D'AMBROSIO

My first encounter with Bill Vance occurred in the fall of 1989, when I entered Boston University's doctoral program in American Studies. Bill was the director of the program and taught the core course in American studies that fall. My experience up to that time was in the field of American art, stemming from my years as a curator for the Fenimore Art Museum. By the end of the semester, however, Bill had opened up a completely new world to me with his broad and inclusive thinking about the connections between American literature and art. The cornerstone of his approach to American studies was his newly published two-volume work, *America's Rome*. I recall thinking at that time what a terrific and important exhibition it would be, and I hoped that someday a museum would pick up on the topic and do it justice.

Now, twenty years after its publication, we are poised to do just that here at the Fenimore. Over the past two years I worked with Bill to shape his ideas into a visual narrative and secure the loans of artworks from a wide variety of museums and private collections. The result is this exhibition and catalogue, with more than 100 paintings illustrating the nineteenth-century American fascination with Rome. Bill graciously allowed us to reprise his title as we strive to bring his 1989 book up-to-date while celebrating its influence on the field over the course of a generation.

Other developments in the years since the publication of *America's Rome* have influenced this project. In 1992 The Museum of Fine Arts, Boston, published Theodore Stebbins' exhibition catalogue *The Lure of Italy*, the most comprehensive treatment of the larger subject of the explorations of the Italian peninsula by American artists. Lesser known has been the meticulous research of John and Mary McGuigan, who have been studying American artists in Italy for the past twenty years. Their work as it relates specifically to Rome is presented here for the first time in print, and we are very grateful to both John and Mary for agreeing to share the fruits of their labors with our audience. Their enthusiasm for this field is boundless and highly contagious, and we are confident that the material they have uncovered and shared herein will in turn influence a generation of scholars to come.

To Bill Vance, and John and Mary McGuigan, I owe a large debt of gratitude for their participation in this project. Likewise, the museum is indebted to the many generous lenders to the exhibition, all of whom are listed on page 122. All of these individuals and institutions have contributed immeasurably to our effort to recreate the nineteenth-century American fascination with Rome, an enchantment that resonates with meaning to this day.

# America's Rome

WILLIAM L. VANCE

Benjamin West, in 1760, was the first American artist to go to Rome to study, to work, and to live. In the course of the next century (and down to the present day) he was followed by scores of other painters, sculptors, and writers. The paintings and statues that they created, and the poems, novels, essays, and dramas that they wrote under the inspiration of that ancient city, have become artifacts of American culture. In the nineteenth century, especially, Rome had both political and aesthetic value for Americans. Politically, Rome—a Republic that became an Empire—was both model and warning. Aesthetically, it continued to offer the same unrivaled sources for picturesque, beautiful, and sublime creations that European painters had found there since the Renaissance. Three particular images of ancient Rome—the Roman Forum, the Colosseum, and the Campagna Romana (the surrounding countryside)—dominated the creative consciousness of the Americans, offering inherently symbolic objects for contemplation and representation.

*Opposite*
Fig. 2. SCENE ON THE
MEDITERRANEAN AFTER
A SHOWER, ca. 1832 (detail)

Thomas Cole (1801–1848)
Oil on wood panel
13¾ x 10⁹⁄₁₆ in. (34.9 x 26.8 cm)
Private collection

*Right*
Fig. 3. ITALIAN
LANDSCAPE, ca. 1805

Washington Allston (1779–1843)
Oil on canvas
40 x 50¾ in. (101.6 x 128.9 cm)
Addison Gallery of American Art,
Phillips Academy, Andover,
Massachusetts. Museum purchase

# The Roman Forum: *History's Largest Page*

In 1849 Jasper F. Cropsey created a rare painting (fig. 4) that places us right in the middle of the ancient Roman Forum. The incredible historical density of the place is immediately apparent. Before us are images from across the millennium during which the Forum was the civic center of the city. Remaining columns of two magnificent temples stand to the left. On the right, we look through an imperial arch of the early third century. Beyond are the huge stones of a building that held the archives of the Roman Republic, now crowned by the central building of the Renaissance city hall designed by Michelangelo. One corner of that retains the fortified papal tower. On the left foreground is an isolated column that was the last structure ever erected here by pagan Rome (608 C.E.). The ramp from the Via Sacra up to the vanished temples that once crowned the

*Below*
Fig. 4. THE ROMAN FORUM. 1849
Jasper F. Cropsey (1823–1900)
Oil on canvas
33 x 51 in. (83.8 x 129.5 cm)
Newington-Cropsey Foundation

*Opposite*
Fig. 5. MARIUS AMID THE RUINS
OF CARTHAGE. 1832
(reduced replica of 1807 version)
John Vanderlyn (1775–1852)
Oil on wood panel
32 x 25⅜ in. (81.2 x 64.4 cm)
Albany Institute of History
& Art. 1946.81

Capitoline Hill, and the buried Rostra, temples, and tombs of the foreground, are trampled by contemporary monks and peasants and their goats, going about their daily business.

In the early nineteenth century the Forum was still known as the Campo Vaccino—the Cow Pasture—and was still used as such; it was also a place for farmers' markets, public laundering, and disposal of refuse. Over the next century (and continuing to the present day), archaeological digs lowered the ground to its original level and exposed the foundations of temples, houses, and large basilicas that now appeared as nothing but rows of marble stumps. The progressive excavations became a gradual revelation of the true character of the Roman

Forum and of its evolution over the several hundred years in which it throbbed as the city's heart. But the ruins of the Forum became only more difficult to interpret, and the fact that they were subject to endless scholarly controversy did not encourage a confident understanding of the site. American painters, unable to see before them the source of the sublime (largely imaginary) compositions of Claude and Poussin and the engravings of Piranesi, tended to avoid the place, and headed for the Campagna. One of them, Rembrandt Peale, wrote in 1830 that he had expected to find in the Forum "crowded groups of picturesque beauty, the charms of ancient art in mighty ruin, combined with the romantic decorations of overgrowing moss and hanging ivy." Instead he saw "fields of dirt and rubbish" and "the scattered monuments of ancient power— the half-buried arch, the isolated column or solitary portico, the masses of brick and mortar; whilst the carved altars, graceful statues, beautiful vases, and elegant columns had all been removed." As a consequence, representation and interpretation of the Forum were left largely to writers. Literary imagination, quite unrestrained by the visual reality, could draw upon familiar classical historians and great romantic poets to create the Forum they desired.

*Six Months in Italy* (1853), by George Stillman Hillard, was for thirty years the most popular American guidebook to Rome. Its approach reflected the sensibility of the classically-educated travelers of the previous half-century. Standing in the tower of the Capitoline Hill, Hillard could admit that what he looked down upon was "a desolation." Nevertheless, he became rapturous over what he could also see: "the history and literature of Rome are lying at our feet, and the living landscape is a page, on which is written half of all that we have learned at school and at college." The metaphor was the common one for the Forum. Nathaniel Hawthorne wrote that the Capitoline tower "looks abroad, upon a larger page, of deeper historic interest, than any other scene can show." The more visionary, as well as the more deeply inspired readers of Latin literature and Byronic poetry, were able to people the Forum with scenes of vital historic significance. The Bostonian George Ticknor, in Rome in 1817 while on a European tour to prepare himself to become America's first scholar-teacher of modern foreign languages and literatures, remarked that in the Forum, where there was "so little to be seen," there was nevertheless "a great deal to be felt and fancied . . . on a spot so full of the past, from the times of Hercules and Evander to our own." The popular journalist Grace Greenwood (Sarah Jane Lippincott), the most exclamatory of visionaries, described in several pages the characters and scenes from Roman history that realized themselves before her eyes in the Forum in 1852. Even a traveler like Bayard Taylor, a Quaker farmer's boy with no formal education who arrived at the Forum in 1845, at the age of twenty, after hiking across Europe by foot, could be equally hallucinatory: There he saw his boyhood dream of "giant, god-like, fallen Rome" come to life in "grandeur" and "splendor inconceivable." What made this possible? Taylor is explicit: the "words of power and glory" that now came back to him. His imagination, fed by the classics, Goethe and Byron, supplied what was literally absent but was not therefore less authentically realized.

The pleasures of these visions are abundantly evident in one of the most attractive and personal accounts from the pre-Civil War period: *Rome: As Seen by a New-Yorker in 1843–44,* by William Gillespie, a civil engineer whose

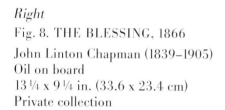

*Right*
Fig. 8. THE BLESSING, 1866
John Linton Chapman (1839–1905)
Oil on board
13 ¼ x 9 ¼ in. (33.6 x 23.4 cm)
Private collection

particularly Roman specialties were road building and land surveying. Remarkably untroubled and joyful, Gillespie is most informative on the subjects of wine and pasta. But he testifies also to the "intense quivering excitement" he felt in the Forum where even his "fingers' ends tingled with enthusiasm . . . . I walked on in solitude through the fields which were once the Forum in which the people met to decide upon the fates of empires, and in which the eloquence of Cicero had re-echoed from the temples and palaces which then studded every eminence and filled every valley." Later, as Gillespie imagines Horace (whom he quotes in Latin) walking along the Via Sacra, he is deeply moved by being able "to tread in his steps." At one spot he imagines the shop "where Virginius bought the knife with which he stabbed his daughter, to save her from Appius Claudius." With reluctance he awakens from the vivid "dream-like sensation" of "standing in the midst of such scenes." Similar envisioning of the past is the very stuff of fiction, in historical romances and in novels with contemporary Rome as a setting. The dénouement of William Ware's very popular romance, *Zenobia* (1838), takes place in the Forum, as the queen of Palmyra is led in chains in Emperor Aurelian's triumph. And in Hawthorne's *The Marble Faun* (1860), as his little quartet of characters marches through the Forum singing "Hail, Columbia!," the narrator conjures up a contrasting ancient Triumph passing through the Arch of Titus and along the Sacred Way.

Exhilarating as the experience of the Forum was to all who could hear what the speaking fragments said in their silent language, its meaning was so entirely dependent upon a prior knowledge of history, philosophy, and poetry as to render the place itself superfluous. Ware himself states that in the end the architectural monuments are not the worthiest of lasting memorials, "magnificent" and "imperishable as they seem." Rome's literature and her Latin language, "wrought . . . into the substance of every living tongue of Europe," are "evidences of her universal sovereignty greater than any other." After the art critic Henry T. Tuckerman stood in the Forum in 1836 and conjured up Cicero's attack upon the Cataline conspirators, he concluded that the "comparative worthlessness of the outward scene" is actually salutary, since it reminds us that "it is the acts themselves, with all their beautiful philosophy, which alone have hallowed these portions of the earth." In the words of George Hillard, where "the eye of the body" could see only an "unsightly piece of ground," the eye of the mind saw a people characterized by "wisdom, valour, and eloquence." So attention naturally turned from the place itself to the uses for the modern American of the Roman political innovations and the moral examples of the Romans.

The idea of the Forum—with its Senate House and its orators' Rostrum—as the place where the Romans established the principles of Law and Liberty, infused much of the political debate in the early years of the American Republic. In the history of the Roman Republic, John Adams found his best proofs that senates were indispensable to democracy. Liberty could be preserved only by limiting the power of the masses, which were easily swayed by demagogues and dictators. But when, in 1839, during the post-Jacksonian period, a young Harvard graduate named Samuel Eliot visited the Forum, he conceived the idea of writing the history of liberty—from its birth in the Forum to its "maturity" in America—with the intention of demonstrating that the growth of liberty coincided with the growth of plebeian power. The patricians alone originally possessed the "rights of liberty and law," he argued, and it was "the good fortune of Rome, that another class of citizens, at first inferior, was included within her fold." To this class the Republic's "elevation and prosperity and freedom [are] to be ascribed." Both Adams and Eliot, from their different political perspectives, agreed that the Roman Republic provided their most positive example of the importance of a balance of power between the "Aristocracy" and the "Democracy." But during the period of the Republic's maturity, which lasted 230 years, "The distinction between patrician and plebeian was become altogether nominal," wrote Adams. "The wisest and most respected of the citizens, from every condition, were raised into office, and the assemblies, whether of the senate or the people, . . . suffered themselves to be governed by the counsels of a few able and virtuous men."

Roman Virtue was legendary in the eighteenth and early nineteenth centuries. More than a few American politicians saw themselves as successors to Cicero, not only as orators but as supreme patriots, the wise and eloquent saviors of their country in moments of crisis. Roman virtues—strength, pride, fortitude, courage, integrity (see fig. 5)—were distinct from the Christian virtues of humility and faith, love and mercy. To contemplate an *exemplum virtutis* was the reason to read most tales from Roman history and literature, which also provided numerous subjects for paintings and statues. Benjamin West took from Tacitus the image of Agrippina returning to Italy with the ashes of her husband Germanicus (Yale University Art Gallery), displaying in her grief the noble comportment expected of aristocratic Roman matrons. West's *The Departure of Regulus* (Her Majesty Queen Elizabeth II) shows an image of self-sacrificial patriotism taken from Livy. Drama, too, served as a didactic form, whether in a popular import like Addison's *Cato* (Washington's favorite play), or an

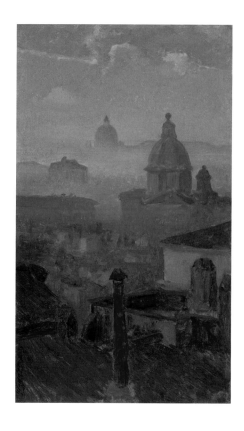

*Below*
Fig. 11. ROMA, 1869
Anne Whitney (1821–1915)
Bronze. 27 x 15 ½ x 20 in.
(68.6 x 39.4 x 50.8 cm)
Gift to the College by the Class of 1886. Davis Museum and Cultural Center, Wellesley College, Wellesley, Massachusetts, 1891.1

16

*Opposite*
Fig. 10. VIEW FROM VIA
SISTINA 72, ROME, ca. 1874
Elihu Vedder (1836–1923)
Oil on canvas
12 ⅝ x 7 ⅝ in. (32 x 19.4 cm)
Private collection

American tragedy by John Howard Payne, *Brutus, or the Fall of Tarquin* (1818), about the founder of the Roman Republic. The hero of Robert Montgomery Bird's *The Gladiator* (1831) is the slave-rebel Spartacus; it makes a passionate attack on an imperial republic based on slavery. In American sculpture one finds countless Founding Fathers and later statesmen dressed in togas—even Andrew Jackson. George Washington, of course, was the chief object of this Romanization of virtuous American heroes by sculptors, from Canova to Horatio Greenough. Philip Freneau proclaimed him "a Roman Hero," and a century later a character in Henry Adams's *Democracy* says to a party visiting Mt. Vernon, "To us he is Morality, Justice, Duty, Truth, half a dozen Roman gods

*Above*
Fig. 12. PINCIAN HILL
(IL PINCIO WITH A VIEW
OF VILLA MEDICI), 1888

Charles Caryl Coleman (1840–1928)
Oil on canvas
22 ½ x 36 ⅞ in. (57.1 x 93.6 cm)
Private collection, Texas

with capital letters." But of all the American writers in Rome, Margaret Fuller was the one most enthusiastically inspired by ancient Roman ideals. As a journalist she worked in Rome during a new phase of its history. She wrote in support of the rise of the People of Rome during the brief period of a new Roman Republic (1848–49, see fig. 6), which was now in its turn inspired by the American example. Fuller had learned Latin as a child; the "thoughts and lives" of the "great Romans" were her "daily food," she later claimed. She learned that "the genius of Rome displayed itself in Character. . . We are never better understood than when we speak of a 'Roman Virtue,' a 'Roman outline.' . . . ROME! It stands by itself, a clear Word. The power of a will, the dignity of a fixed purpose, is what it utters."

# The Colosseum: *Ambiguities of Empire*

> Thus fell the mistress of the conquer'd earth
> Great ROME, who ow'd to ROMULUS her birth,
> Fell to the monster Luxury a prey,
> Who forc'd a hundred nations to obey.
> —Philip Freneau, "The American Village" (1772)

The most familiar of all Roman sights has always been the Colosseum: constantly described, painted both as a landscape ruin and as the backdrop for portraiture, and employed as a symbolic element in fiction. A magnificent architectural wonder, it had been historically the scene of the most violent entertainments and, legendarily, of Christian martyrdoms. It represented the Roman Empire during the centuries of greatest power and greatest decadence. It stood for what the Republic became. Did it also forewarn of what America might become? Freneau himself feared so, ending "The American Village" by warning that America might also "decay" from the vice of Luxury, as had Rome. If it did, he said, "The world itself must fall as well as she."

The cumulative, complex American image of the Colosseum expresses an ambivalent attitude toward imperial power: its rise, its glories and terrors, and its fall. The Colosseum becomes the Moby-Dick of architecture, a sublimely multivalent symbol, sacred yet malignant, alien and dreadful yet magnificent, ravaged yet enduring.

When viewed most simply as an architectural ruin that has virtually become a landscape, it is seen as an object of melancholy beauty. Of the many American painters, mostly forgotten, who painted the Colosseum, Thomas Cole is the most important. Cole considered it the most affecting of the "wondrous things" of Rome. His verbal description in his notebook of 1832 opens with the same perspective adopted in the small canvas (fig. 17) probably painted in the same year:

*Below*

Fig. 13. THE COLOSSEUM, 1832
Francis Alexander (1800–1880)
Pen and ink on buff wove paper,
bound in a sketchbook
Sketchbook dimensions:
7 x 10 ½ in. (17.7 x 26.6 cm)
Private collection

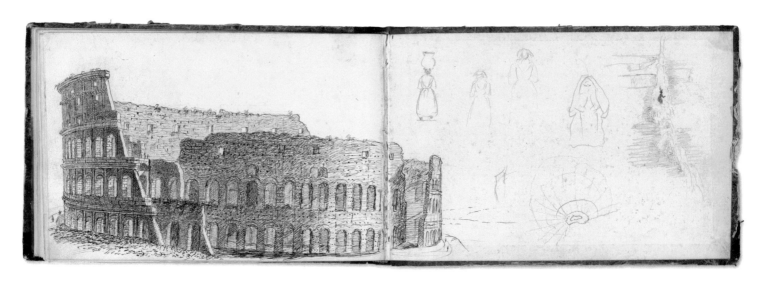

It is stupendous, yet beautiful in its destruction. From the broad arena within, it rises around you, arch above arch, broken and desolate, and mantled in many parts with the laurustinus, the acanthus, and numerous other plants and flowers. . . . It looks more like a work of nature than of man, for the regularity of art is lost . . . .

*Above*

Fig. 14. SELF PORTRAIT, 1860/1861

William Page (1811–1885)

Oil on canvas

59 x 36 in. (149.9 x 91.4 cm)

Gift of Mr. and Mrs. George S. Page,
Blinn S. Page, Lowell Briggs Page and
Mrs. Leslie Stockton Howell

The Detroit Institute of Arts, 37.60

*Above*

Fig. 15. MRS. WILLIAM PAGE, 1860/1861

William Page (1811–1885)

Oil on canvas

60 ¼ x 36 ¼ in. (153 x 92.1 cm)

Gift of Mr. and Mrs. George S. Page,
Blinn S. Page, Lowell Briggs Page and
Mrs. Leslie Stockton Howell

The Detroit Institute of Arts, 37.61

*Above*

Fig. 16. BATHS OF
CARACALLA, 1841

John William Casilear (1811–1893)
Graphite heightened with
white gouache on tan wove paper
7¾ x 7¾ in. (19.7 x 19.7 cm)
Private collection

Similar descriptions are found in the writings of Henry James, Herman Melville, Bayard Taylor, William Wetmore Story, and George Hillard. They all manage to see the Colosseum as a romantic reclamation by Nature. When archeological excavations began to reveal the bare bones of its interior, travelers were outraged. Its picturesque and sublime aspects were being destroyed.

At the opposite extreme from this perception of the Colosseum as a sublime mountain was the attempt to re-create it, visually and verbally, as it was at the time of the Empire. The historical realism of Gérôme, who painted several scenes of sport and martyrdom in the Colosseum, inspired a series of detailed paintings in the 1870s by Edwin Howland Blashfield that eschewed the heroic to emphasize decadence. Earlier, when in Rome in the 1830s, Cole had conceived his famous *Course of Empire* series (New-York Historical Society), which begins with the "savage" state and proceeds through the "consummation" of empire to end in "desolation." The painting called *Consummation*, the central panel of the series, is highly ambiguous. It shows a gorgeous triumphal arrival at a port from which monumental architecture has eliminated all natural contours. Is this luxurious world being celebrated or deplored? Is it proposed as the goal or the inevitable fate of America? In the last decade of the century, the "White City" of the Columbian World's Fair in Chicago, which resembled the *Consummation*, provoked similar questions. On the banks of Lake Michigan in 1893, Henry Adams felt himself back on the steps of the Capitoline in Rome, asking questions about historical sequences, for which he had only pessimistic answers.

Other writers did not worry so much. Grace Greenwood was thrilled to imagine Christian martyrdoms, hearing lions "roaring and bounding beneath me." Mark Twain delighted in drawing up a complete playbill for a "General Slaughter," sarcastically recalling the Catholic Inquisition as equivalent to the ancient Roman tortures. And Margaret Fuller went so far as to sympathize with the "fierce excitements" of "fights of men and lions" in the ancient arenas as indications of life intensely lived. To her, now far from the genteel confines of Concord and Boston, violence and sacrifice were expressive elements within a larger life conceived on the imperious scale worthy of Man.

Looking at the astonishing engineering achievement of the Colosseum, Timothy Dwight had already asked, in 1821, "When the human power has reached this point, where shall the limit be placed?" The enormous scale of ancient monuments, the genius of their construction, and the imperial associations they bore, all should have made contemporary individuals realize their comparative insignificance. "The greatest men of the age scarcely bore the test of posing with Rome for a background," wrote Henry Adams. "Perhaps Garibaldi—possibly even Cavour," he allowed, and from the past Tacitus, Michelangelo, and "at a pinch," Gibbon. But one "hardly saw a Napoleon III there, or Palmerston, or Tennyson, or Longfellow." Had Adams perhaps seen the painting of Longfellow and his daughter, doll-like figures standing beneath the Arch of Titus with the Colosseum in the background? George Healy, Frederic Church, and James McEntee did not intend to be satirical in their circa 1871 collaborative painting, *The Arch of Titus* (The Newark Museum), for they included themselves in the right foreground, one of them sketching the complacent Longfellows (who had had themselves photographed in this pose). A century earlier John Singleton Copley had painted *Mr. and Mrs. Ralph Izard* (Museum of Fine Arts, Boston), in which the Colosseum is reduced to a small landscape element in the center background, visible from the loggia of a

sumptuous villa. The great arena becomes a tiny aesthetic indicator of the glorious city in which the Izards, comparatively monumental, complacently find themselves. In contrast, in William Page's portrait of his wife (fig. 15), the perspective is such as to make the self-assured Mrs. Page commensurate with the monument. She in fact appears more sturdy, more noble than the Colosseum, and in her own way as beautiful and imposing.

Thus the three most familiar American portraits showing the Colosseum have aggrandizing, diminishing, and equalizing effects on the American figures who appear before it. In literature the relations are more complex, but the figures are from a narrower range. Madwomen and geniuses populate much of the minor writing of the time, such as novels by Theodore S. Fay and Washington Allston, and revelatory scenes tend to occur in the Colosseum. The ruin's appeal to extreme states of mind had been established by Byron; it was exploited by Poe, who by reading Byron did not even need to go to Rome to catch the fever. Major fiction is more nuanced in its presentation of the arena's effects. Hawthorne's *The Marble Faun* and Henry James's *Roderick Hudson* and *The Portrait of a Lady* all exploit the multifaceted challenge to the human spirit made by the Colosseum. Most famously, James's *Daisy Miller* ends with the young American girl dying of Roman fever after a moonlight stroll with a young Italian. "Well, I *have* seen the Colosseum by moonlight," she says. "That's one thing I can rave about!" James's tale might be seen as his first attempt to see how much dignity and importance could be attributed to the presumptively small and unaware, like an American girl. His answer is ambiguous, but like all of James's characters who respond to the Emersonian injunction to descend into the dust of the arena to take the measure of themselves—"She would have appreciated one's esteem."

From the beginning of the American Republic, there had been poets—David Humphreys and Timothy Dwight among them—who argued that Rome, as a Republic that had become an Empire, served only as a negative model for America, a dire warning. By the beginning of the twentieth century, Henry Adams could see our own Civil War as ancient history, and write that Americans had become "as familiar with political assassination as though they had lived under Nero. The climax of empire could be seen approaching, year after year, as though Sulla were a President or McKinley a Consul."

The ultimate meaning—or non-meaning—of the Colosseum was summed up with astonishing power by Longfellow himself in a fragment from his verse drama *Michael Angelo* (1882), in which he imagines the great sculptor meeting a companion in the Colosseum. The genius has come there to "learn" lessons of beauty from the "great master of antiquity" who designed it. His friend objects that the arena once served "people / Whose pleasure was the pain of dying men." Michelangelo replies that Nature has reclaimed it, and in this also it is capable of teaching lessons of beauty. But Longfellow does not stop with this familiar uniting of Art, History, and Nature in the building's identity. His Michelangelo then converts the Colosseum into a philosophical symbol. An apocalyptic vision of the world's dissolution ends with the words: "Naught but the core of the great globe remained, / A skeleton of stone."

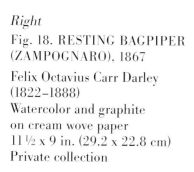

*Right*
Fig. 18. RESTING BAGPIPER
(ZAMPOGNARO), 1867

Felix Octavius Carr Darley
(1822–1888)
Watercolor and graphite
on cream wove paper
11 ½ x 9 in. (29.2 x 22.8 cm)
Private collection

## The Campagna Romana: *Silence Made Visible*

In the spring of 1833 America's first "foreign correspondent" stood on the "lofty turrets" of the Tomb of Cecilia Metella and saw before him the original of "one of the finest landscapes ever painted"—Thomas Cole's "picture of the Roman Campagna": "the long aqueducts stretching past, . . . forming a chain of noble arches from Rome to the mountains of Albano." The oil was hardly dry on the work that N.P. Willis so confidently rated; it had been painted the year before. A second version of the same scene, painted by Cole in 1843 after another visit to Rome (Wadsworth Athenaeum), is described by William Cullen Bryant in his funeral oration for Cole in 1848 as one of the pictures "which we most value and most affectionately admire . . . with its broad masses of shadow dividing the sunshine that bathes the solitary plain strewn with ruins, its glorious mountains in the distance and its silence made visible to the eye."

The Claudian aqueduct was the ruin on the Campagna most popular with American artists who stopped in Rome in the nineteenth century. But the paintings by George Loring Brown, Jasper Cropsey, Sanford Robinson Gifford, John Rollin Tilton, and George Inness all lack Cole's drama of light and dark.

*Above*
Fig. 19. ITALIAN SCENE, COMPOSITION, 1833
Thomas Cole (1801–1848)
Oil on canvas
27 ½ x 54 ½ in. (69.8 x 138.4 cm)
Collection of The New-York Historical Society, 1858.19

23

Other things they necessarily have in common, with the Coles and with each other. Inherently pictorial qualities are provided by the diminishing perspective of the aqueduct, the vertical thrust of its arches in opposition to the wide undulating spaces of the Campagna, and the rough texture of the plain contrasting with the softly glowing sky that typically occupies nearly half of the canvas. From Cole to Inness (in a tradition that went back through Richard Wilson and others to Claude Lorrain), the Campagna made a powerful aesthetic appeal, in its light and in the simple geometries of its forms—aqueducts, tombs, towers, and trees—defined by that light against the low straight horizon of the sea or the gently swelling cones of hills. Equally important, those forms and those hills and the very ground itself had inherent historical and literary value. Most of the artists who went to Rome did so in the belief that a painter was a poet and a historian and a moralist, and that Rome was the inspiration and school for this humanistic tradition in art. For over half a century Americans joined other landscape artists from the North in the task of representing the beauty and interpreting the meaning of the Campagna and its adjacent

*Above*
Fig. 21. THE ROMAN
CAMPAGNA, 1859

Sanford Robinson Gifford (1823–1880)
Oil on canvas
6 x 10 ⅛ in. (15.2 x 25.7 cm)
The Frances Lehman Loeb Art Center,
Vassar College, Poughkeepsie, New York,
Gift of Matthew Vassar, 1864.1.34

*Below*
Fig. 22. AQUEDUCTS
OF THE CAMPAGNA, 1859

Thomas Worthington
Whittredge (1820–1910)
Oil on canvas
33 x 53¾ in. (83.8 x 136.5 cm)
Cincinnati Art Museum,
Bequest of Caroline Hooper, 1900.1

hills. In their company were American writers of all kinds who in their own medium participated in the final representation of the Campagna before it lost forever the appearance that had made it seem a symbol of time, itself become timeless.

Whatever the Campagna's inherent aesthetic potential, the essential point is that it was not just any landscape. In Mme. De Staël's celebrated Roman novel *Corinne* (1807), widely read by Americans going to Rome, they found a clear assertion of the prevailing view: the "singular charm" of the Campagna was owing to its having in abundance precisely what America lacked. "The most beautiful countries in the world, when they bring to mind no recollections, when they bear the stamp of no remarkable event, are stripped of interest." A landscape dotted with ruins inevitably bore associations, and became an edifying symbol: the ruins "present the image of time, which has made them what they are." The silence made visible in the paintings of the Campagna is not the silence of the virgin American wilderness that most of these artists also painted. It is a silence that recalls dead voices, just as the "vacancy" of the Campagna is a reminder of lost plenitude. In the paintings of the Claudian aqueduct by Cole and Gifford and Cropsey, the marvelous engineering feat of Roman civilization that carried the sustaining water of life into the great city *seems* to be, like time itself, without beginning or end as it enters into the picture on one side and disappears on the other. But the reality lies in the ravages at the center of the scene and in the utter desolation that spreads around them.

*Above*
Fig. 25. ITALIAN LANDSCAPE, 1839
Thomas Cole (1801–1848)
Oil on canvas
36 x 53 in. (91.44 x 134.6 cm)
Collection of The Butler Institute
of American Art, Youngstown, Ohio.
Museum Purchase, 1945

James calls the Campagna a "wilderness"—the common word for *American* nature; and so, like the savage state of the American landscape, it required the artist to give it expressive form. There was a vacancy to be filled and a silence to be made eloquent.

Painters and writers responded by evoking two contradictory visions. One is melancholy and moralistic, the other pastoral and transcendent. On the one hand they present the wasteland of former civilizations, what Hillard called a "historical palimpsest" in which nature has nearly covered over the ruins of one civilization, the Roman, which had conquered and buried another, the

*Right*
Fig. 26. TOR DE' SCHIAVI, 1873
David Maitland Armstrong
(1836–1918)
Oil on canvas
14 5/8 x 29 5/8 in. (37.1 x 75.2 cm)
Private collection

27

*Above*
Fig. 27. SOUVENIR OF ITALY, 1874
George Inness (1825–1894)
Oil on canvas
20¾ x 30½ in. (50.8 x 76.2 cm)
Howard Gotlieb Archival Research
Center, Boston University

Etruscan. As such it is a place of "desolate and tragic beauty," "inseparably connected with the ideal image of Rome, . . . vocal with so many voices of wisdom and warning." In this view, the Campagna is essentially an emblem of mutability and a *memento mori*. On the other hand, the primitivism of the present scene—the shepherds with their dogs, the goats and the sheep and the buffaloes, the inducements to mirthful idleness on picnics in the verdant villas of Albano, or the evocations of rural serenity at Horace's farm near Tivoli, with the Campagna below stretching toward Rome or to the sea—all these images and ideas stirred writers and painters toward an exactly opposing vision: the illusion of an accessible Arcadia beyond the city walls, as in Vergil's poetry, a bosky place beyond the actions of time. Thus the Campagna was read both as historical desert and as eternal garden. Generally these antithetical images are kept as distinct from each other as Eden from the fallen world, but as contraries they inevitably suggest and confront each other. Even in Vergil, Arcadia is violated by dispossession and death.

# The Wasteland

To the young scholar George Ticknor in 1817, nothing was more "heartrending" than the "boundless waste" of the Campagna. In 1845, tramping across the Campagna, Bayard Taylor saw it as an "accursed" landscape: amidst the signs of a ruined civilization, a few shepherds looked "wild and savage enough for any kind of crime." The tomb-bordered Via Appia filled travelers like James Fenimore Cooper and Timothy Dwight with fear and thoughts of Death. In many fictions, most notably Hawthorne's *The Marble Faun* (1865), a descent into the catacombs beneath the Campagna's fields accentuates its morbidity. A painting made in 1869 of the Via Appia by John Linton Chapman (fig. 127) is almost surreal in its exclusive focus on the sun-baked and misshapen remains of the tombs along a road that seems endless. Only a few paintings by Inness, also done in the 1870s, convey a similar sense of utter depletion, of minimal persistence of life under a too-hot sun and upon a barren ground among bleached ruins. Other paintings convey that "passion for excavation" that grew throughout the century, by suggesting the evidences of former life that once thrived beyond the walls of Rome: fragments of villas and temples, mosaic pavements, unearthed

statues. But no matter how diligently archaeologists dug things up, or how luxuriantly Nature covered them over and pushed herself forward in their place, what one beheld remained fundamentally a vacancy suggesting lost plenitude. In *Art and Nature in Italy* (1882), the artist Eugene Benson summed up the image of the Campagna as wasteland: "Something ghostly, phantom-like, great, formless, vague, seems to be a presence by day and by night on the Campagna, oppressing the mind and filling it with melancholy disquiet. It is a homeless space of mighty memories. Fever and death here watch and slay through centuries of life."

*Above*

Fig. 29. THE CASCATELLI, TIVOLI, LOOKING TOWARDS ROME, ca. 1832

Thomas Cole (1801–1848)
Oil on canvas
32¾ x 44½ in. (83.2 x 113 cm)
Columbus Museum of Art, Ohio
Gift of Mr. and Mrs. Walter Knight
Sturges and Family, 1991.013.001

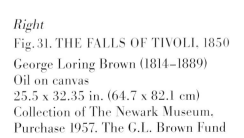

# Arcadia

Realization of the Campagna's actual desolation stimulated the search for its opposite. Sometimes the competing images provide the drama within a painting or a passage of prose. Two paintings by Inness (including fig. 20) show a tree-shaded dwelling on the edge of a barren plain defined by a waterless aqueduct. The same opposition between wasteland and shady home is evident in writers' descriptions of journeys across the Campagna to Tivoli, Frascati, and Albano, where they reach an Arcadia beyond and above the historical desert of death. Eugene Benson records the sensations of a three-hour drive in the evening from Rome up to Lake Nemi. A point midway on the Campagna, and the arrival at Nemi, indicate the psychic distance travelled:

> We have passed the old Via Latina, with a few tombs yet standing, but in ruin, and are now in the midst of the wide waste and beauty and silence of the Roman Campagna. ...Close by we see the whitened and withered stocks of the asphodel. ...The spectral moon rises above Monte Cavo.
>
> But within an hour we were at Nemi, ...under luxuriant tasseled foliage of chestnut, and beech, and the darker-leaved ilex; and on each side of the road we saw ivy of Bacchus, and jessamine, and clematis and honeysuckle vines, which here trail in tangled lavishness, lighted by the moon. The night-owl cried from depths of darkness across the lake. ...Could it be a fact that great Rome was but three hours away? We were now in the very bosky places of old mythology.

Benson painted two pictures of the lake, which he dedicated to "the poet-artist, Gifford," whose sunset view of Lake Nemi (Toledo Museum of Art) had first given him an idea of this sacred place.

*Above*
Fig. 32. THE CITADEL
AT PALESTRINA, 1857 (detail)

Peter Frederick Rothermel
(1812–1895)
Oil on pale gray wove paper
11 x 8 ¼ in. (27.9 x 20.9 cm)
Private collection

*Right*
Fig. 33. CONVENT
AT FRASCATI, 1856

George Inness (1825–1894)
Oil on canvas
21 ½ x 29 ¾ in. (54.6 x 75.5 cm)
Private collection

*Above*
Fig. 34. FOUNTAIN AT
PALESTRINA, 1850
Thomas Hicks (1823–1890)
Oil on canvas
24 ½ x 31 in. (62.2 x 78.7 cm)
Private collection

Writers and painters alike tended to move away from the wasteland toward the Arcadian ideal, derived from the poetry of Vergil and the paintings of Claude. Arcadia is populated. While Americans very rarely followed Claude in placing gods or mythological figures in their landscapes, they were pleased to meet their patrons' demands for happy country people who dance, tend their sheep, and meditate while sitting on ruins. What was wanted was an image of nature and man in perfect harmony.

Yet the writers all knew that the real pastoral life of the Campagna was anything but idyllic, and they admit that their hill-town retreats are actually "squalid" and "miserable," the very opposite of an industrious New England

*Above*
Fig. 35. PEASANT FAMILY, 1867
Felix Octavius Carr Darley
(1822–1888)
Watercolor and graphite
on cream wove paper
13 3/16 x 17 1/2 in. (33.4 x 44.4 cm)
Private collection

village. The painting that comes closest to suggesting that the Campagna could be seen as something other than either wasteland or idyllic garden is John Gadsby Chapman's *Harvesters on the Roman Campagna*, executed in at least three versions in the 1860s (one of which is in the Yale University Art Gallery). Such a realistic contemporary scene of labor is, as Benson noted, "beautiful and inspiriting to look at." But Hillard's extensively researched account of the actual life of these harvesters states that "we have no right to look upon a landscape only as a picture, or to view it merely as a harvest-field for dreamy emotions or fine visions." The reality is that some "enormous capitalists" (including Prince Borghese and two branches of the Church—the St. Peter's Corporation and the Hospital of Santo Spirito) have title to all the land, which yields "a miserable pittance to a population wasted by toil and paralyzed by poverty." By the end of

34

the season, only half of these itinerant workers will remain alive. "The beauty of the Campagna . . . is turned to ashes."

There was no occasion for disillusionment in this, since all knew that what they sought was an aesthetic ideal, not the reality of Italy. Artists, writers, and patrons only wanted an Arcadia of art, or else believed that as a necessity of history the Golden Age was in the future and the "real" Arcadia was in the West. Stumbling sometimes upon what seemed momentarily to be Arcadia in the present day was a wonderful boon. At Viterbo, north of Rome, Willis and his companion just before daylight "heard music in the street, and looking out at the door, we saw a long procession of young girls, dressed with flowers in their hair, and each playing a kind of cymbal, and dancing as she went along. . . . It was like a train of Corybantes. . . . They were going out to pluck the last grapes. The whole thing was poetical, and in keeping, for Italy."

## Five Personal Campagnas

For many American writers and artists, the encounter with the Roman Campagna inspired the expression of their own aesthetic, psychological, and spiritual place. Five artists in particular created important works related to that encounter. Here I can only suggest, by way of conclusion, their principal themes and forms.

*Below*

Fig. 36. CASTLE GANDOLFO, LAKE ALBANO, ITALY, 1852

Christopher Pearse Cranch (1813–1892)

Oil on canvas

36 ½ x 54 ½ in. (92.7 x 138.4 cm)

Corcoran Gallery of Art, Washington, D.C. Gift of William Wilson Corcoran, 69.23

*Above*

Fig. 37. PORTRAIT OF A
CONTADINA, ca. 1853
John Whetten Ehninger (1827–1889)
Charcoal and white chalk on paper
27 x 26 in. (68.5 x 66 cm)
Private collection

*Above*

Fig. 38. ITALIAN WOMAN, ca. 1852
George Augustus Baker Jr.
(1821–1880)
Oil on canvas
27 x 22 in. (68.5 x 55.8 cm)
Private collection

About a quarter of the 200 paintings of Washington Allston are related to his experience of Italy, early in the century. He found there the validation of his romantic dream. The actual Campagna provided sensuous sources for the "forms of Truth" he sought to create, inspired by those achieved in works by Claude and (especially) Poussin. Allston's beautiful landscapes (fig. 3), in which both buildings and representative people exist in harmony with Nature, provided the "objective correlative" (his term) for a harmonious spiritual state in artist and viewer. Allston's paintings are serene (there is no wasteland) and serious (there are no dancing shepherds). They offer transcendence.

The paintings of Thomas Cole are deeply conflicted. The splendid *Italian Scene, Composition* (fig. 19) is filled with contraries. The image of dancing peasants is balanced by that of the young man who sits on a ruin and meditates. This duality in the Campagna—meditation and dance—is also reflected in Cole's tendency to paint pictures in pairs: *L'Allegro* with *Il Penseroso* (1845, Los Angeles County Museum of Art), for instance—and there are many others, some of them opposing Italian and American pastoral landscapes. In the famous *Course of Empire* (1836) (conceived while Cole sat upon a Roman ruin) the oppositions multiply: *The Arcadian State* vs. *Consummation of Empire* (filled with dancers in a Triumph), both of these opposed to the final work: *Desolation*, the image that owes most to the contemporary Campagna (see study, fig. 101).

In the middle of the century Nathaniel Hawthorne exploited similar antinomies in *The Marble Faun*, in which "golden light" vies with "malarial shade" as the symbol of ultimate truth. In scenes in the Villa Borghese or out in the full Campagna, the idea of Arcadia—the timeless land of innocent fauns—is evoked as an Allston-like dream, an alternative to the reality of the fallen world of sin and death.

In the 1870s George Inness and Henry James arrived at the most original responses to the Campagna. Inness, by this time a firm believer in Swedenborgianism, deemphasized the ruins and classical associations (figs. 20, 23 and 27). An occasional solitary shepherd or monk is shown nearly lost in the natural world of plants, rocks, water, sky, and animals (sheep and cows). Arranged in subtle geometries, these visible elements stand in "correspondence" to the invisible spiritual world, the true reality for Inness. Trees in particular, from the homely ancient olives to the soaring black masses of umbrella pines, are assembled into sacred groves. Bands of color on the plain and in the sky measure off the harmony that underlies everything in Nature. In over a hundred canvases from the Campagna or its adjacent hill-towns of Tivoli and Albano, Inness created his own vision of the Truth. Art and religion are united by "the science of geometry." For Inness, "landscape" was "a continued repetition of the same thing in a different form and in a different feeling." To move from one of Inness's paintings of the Campagna to another is to experience this.

In the same years that Inness was making these visionary discoveries, Henry James was also measuring "the deep delight of knowing the Campagna." On long horseback rides, "I saw more things than I can easily tell." Subsequently he was able to tell much, in the several moving scenes in his Roman stories and novels that occur in the Campagna. But the most extensive and original response actually comes at the beginning, in a long essay (1873) for the *Atlantic Monthly*. To James, the endless horizons, the winding watercourses, the pleasing undulations of the topography, together with the intense historical suggestiveness of the city walls, the tomb-bordered ancient highways, the collapsed villas, and, finally, the deeply sad remnants of pastoral life that one came upon

Fig. 39. EFFECT NEAR NOON—
ALONG THE APPIAN WAY, 1858

George Loring Brown (1814–1889)
Oil on canvas
68 ½ x 96 in. (174 x 243.8 cm)
Spanierman Gallery, New York, NY

in scattered farmhouses—all of these became a symbol of the "illimitable experience" that life offers, nowhere more than in Rome. A ride on the Campagna is "the most romantic of all your possibilities." It challenges you to envision the totality of the unfolding complex experience of Rome and to hold it in a unified "after-vision." When this youthfully lyrical essay is read as preliminary to the tragic evocations of the Campagna in *The Portrait of a Lady* (1881), one sees how a great writer had a vision and found a style that could encompass both romantic idealism and historical realism (both Allston and Hawthorne), both free invention and disciplined representation, both the beautiful reality of innocence and the fact of its inevitable loss.

*This essay is a brief summary of the arguments and analyses of the first three chapters of my* America's Rome, Volume I: Classical Rome *(New Haven, 1989: Yale University Press), where documentation and a full bibliography may also be found.*

# "This Market of Physiognomy"
## American Artists and Rome's Art Academies, Life Schools, and Models, 1825–1870

MARY K. McGUIGAN

*The artists visit this market of physiognomy,*
*disturbing the lazy set who lie lounging on the steps to be hired,*
*but are too idle to rise and show themselves.*
*Here he may pick out the figure and face which best suit his picture.*
—William Gardiner, *Sights in Italy*

Numerous Americans participated in Rome's diverse array of art academies and life schools and interacted with its professional community of models throughout the nineteenth century, a fact that has seldom been acknowledged, much less systematically addressed, by historians of the field. Interest in working from the living model was not limited to devotees of figural art—those sculptors, portraitists, and painters of history, religious, allegorical, and fancy pictures whose livelihoods depended on anatomical correctness, physical likeness, and expression. Many American landscapists, too, attended in the evenings after working outdoors during the day and occasionally hired models to come to their studios. The accessibility and affordability of the establishments in Rome that nightly provided a variety of men, women, and children posed in drapery, Italian regional dress, period costume, or in the nude prompted many landscape specialists to take advantage of them, whether or not they incorporated figures into their final paintings of Italian scenery.

Whether minor accessories within elaborately conceived landscapes or prominent actors in genre scenes, history paintings, and the like, Italian people appeared frequently in nineteenth-century American paintings and sculptures. Beyond their picturesqueness, Henry Theodore Tuckerman (1813–71), the leading American art critic of the period, perhaps best expressed their appeal:

> To the traveler, who cherishes Italian memories, there is somewhat of the poetry of life in a "Beggar-Child," who looks as if he had just stepped out from an angle of the Piazza di Spagna or the shadow of Trajan's Column, so much of the physiognomy and the magnetism of the clime are incarnated in form, complexion, attitude, eye, and expression.[1]

*Left*
Fig. 40. COSTUME PICTURE, 1857 (detail)
James Edward Freeman (1808–1884)
Oil on canvas
59 3/16 x 45 1/2 in. (150.3 x 115.5 cm)
Private collection. See fig. 91.

That the inhabitants of a place somehow embody or assume the attributes of the climatic and geographic conditions peculiar to it may strike us as odd today, but it was a commonly held belief ever since Charles Montesquieu (1689–1755) published his influential meteorological climate theory in 1748. While Tuckerman's contemporaries would have understood his comment within that context, subsequent historians of American art have failed to acknowledge the relevance of his—and Montesquieu's—assertion. In discussing landscapes of Italy painted by nineteenth-century Americans in her 1972 essay "Arcady Revisited," Barbara Novak stated that "what figures were included were generally small . . . and so much a part of the landscape, so thoroughly accommodated to the image, that we are not especially aware of their presence," and she concluded that the artists "felt no special need to excuse their preoccupation with the landscape."[2] I would argue, however, that the figures that struck her as inconspicuous and inconsequential would have been perceived by their original audience as indispensable organic offshoots of the landscape—of Italy—itself.[3] While it is not within the scope of this essay to discuss all the works in this exhibition that contain human figures, it is sincerely hoped that it will inform our understanding of the history of working from the living model and resituate American artists within the vibrant international milieu centered in Rome in the nineteenth century.

## The English Academy

"I must ever remember with gratitude that the English artists then in Rome gave me the advantage of studying in their life school," the New York painter Robert Walter Weir (1803–89) recalled of his brief Roman sojourn from 1825 to 1827.[4] At the invitation of his British colleagues—including the sculptors Richard Westmacott Jr. (1775–1856), Richard Wyatt (1795–1850), and John Gibson (1790–1866); and the painters David Wilkie (1785–1841), Charles Lock Eastlake (1793–1865), and Joseph Severn (1793–1879)—Weir, with his roommate and compatriot, the neoclassical sculptor Horatio Greenough (1805–52), counted among the earliest attendees of the so-called English Academy, established in Rome as recently as 1821. The discipline of drawing, painting, or sculpting nightly from the living model alongside one's peers complemented the other opportunities for improvement that Rome afforded the student of art.

The stated objective of the English Academy was to work from the living model "unimpeded by the inconvenience of attending crowded Schools, and being indebted to the liberality of foreign institutions."[5] Thus, the appellation "academy" was a somewhat curious choice, since it may have been more accurately described as a life school, except that it did also provide "casts, books, and other necessary means of art."[6] The name, moreover, invited comparison with the French Academy in Rome, founded by King Louis XIV more than one hundred and fifty years earlier. But, as an 1823 letter to the editor of the *London Literary Gazette* made clear, the intention was never to "attempt so impossible and undesirable a thing as a rival" to that august, but stagnant, institution:

Impossible, because its necessary funds could not be raised by subscription, and undesirable, as it leaves nothing to the energies and
devotion of the Artists themselves, who, sent out and maintained
there by their Government, have produced nothing since its estab-
lishment worth a tithe of its expense.[7]

In contrast, the English Academy professed greater autonomy and liberality as it relied on public funding, encouraged amateurs, and cost nothing to attend. Yet another notable feature of the English Academy was that they welcomed American painters and sculptors into their ranks. Considering that they sought acknowledgment as a "National Academy" in Rome, and did not themselves want to feel beholden to other countries' largesse, this generosity of spirit is truly remarkable.[8]

Weir and Greenough were the first Americans who we can confirm studied under the English Academy's auspices. While it was only a short walk from their rooms on the Pincian Hill to the English Academy, it probably seemed like entering another world. According to the English painter Edward Villiers Rippingille (1798–1859), one approached it on a "narrow dirty lane, called *Vicolo del Gallinaccio*, or Turkey-cock Alley":

> Passing thence you enter another *via* or *vicolo* worse than the first, and then, in a kind of corner, looking something like a deserted barn, you find the English Academy. It was once a small chapel, but, ruined and desecrated, it has come to its present use. It consists of one room only, which contains a skeleton, an anatomical figure in plaster, a broken cast of the Apollo, and—nothing else, I believe, except a stove, a large *Fuscone* for burning charcoal, a table for the model, and sundry odd-looking desks, benches, stands, and seats for the pupils.[9]

Rippingille thus substantiated that the English Academy was housed in the deconsecrated chapel of San Giovanni della Ficozza (fig. 41), located at Via dei Maroniti 29, near the Roman Academy of St. Luke. This former seat of the Maronite religious order had hosted the English Academy since at least 1823, and, prior to that, it had been home to Joseph Severn. Most histories erroneously place the English Academy from its inception at Via Margutta 53B, where it did eventually move.[10]

Sessions at the English Academy lasted from seven until nine o'clock, the culmination of a busy day that may have otherwise included drawing from casts of antique statuary at the French Academy, making copies after the old masters in the Vatican or another art gallery, creating original paintings in the studio, or working outdoors. It was while steadily improving his craft in Rome that Weir undertook a series of figure sketches for several ambitious compositions that would help to cement his reputation as one of America's preeminent painters. In addition to *Presentation in the Temple* (1835, Private collection), the genesis of Weir's *Taking the Veil* (1863, Yale University Art Gallery) dates to this period, based upon the "consecration of a nun, at which ceremony I was present," the artist wrote.[11]

George Cooke (1793–1849), a native of Maryland, was the next American documented to have studied at the English Academy during his year-and-a-half residency in Rome, from October 1827 to June 1829. A fellow countryman, Lt. John Farley (1803–74), met Cooke in his final year there and commented that he had "attained considerable reputation among the students and artists of the English Academy at Rome."[12] Farley, himself a trained draftsman commissioned by the U.S. government to investigate the latest advances in map making and lithography in Europe, gained access to the English Academy through Cooke and recorded his impressions of it:

*Above left*

Fig. 43. CONTADINA WITH
A DISTAFF, ca. 1828

John Gadsby Chapman (1808–1889)
Watercolor on cream wove paper
14 1/4 x 9 3/4 in. (36.1 x 24.7 cm)
Private collection

*Above right*

Fig. 44. CONTADINO OF
THE CAMPAGNA, ca. 1828

John Gadsby Chapman (1808–1889)
Watercolor on cream wove paper
14 1/4 x 9 3/4 in. (36.1 x 24.7 cm)
Private collection

This is an interesting exhibition. The room is usually darkened, and
the artists are arranged in a semicircle, each with his lamp and his
drawing desk. The person, whether male or female, is placed in the
center of the group and made to assume any attitude upon which
the majority will determine. The light is then admitted from a lamp
above the person, so as to show all the developments of the figure—
its muscles, action, attitude, etc., and its brilliant points. Each one
has a different aspect or point of view, and the sculptors make their
clay models at the same time.[13]

Unfortunately, none of Cooke's output from the English Academy has surfaced
(although some of his copies after the antique have).

Cooke undoubtedly introduced John Gadsby Chapman (1808–89), the portraitist from Virginia to whom he was related by marriage, to the English
Academy upon the latter man's arrival in Rome in 1828. It was in writing
about Chapman that William Dunlap (1766–1839), a fellow painter and the
annalist of this period of American art, stated that models sometimes posed in
the nude before the group assembled at the English Academy. While no examples of this kind by Chapman's hand are known, we do have three costume
studies in watercolor by him that almost certainly date from this early point

in his career: *Seated Contadina Fixing Her Hair Ribbons*, *Contadina with a Distaff*, and *Contadino of the Campagna* (figs. 42–44). Little emphasis has been placed upon conveying a sense of depth or foreshortening in these three frontal views of full-length figures in fairly static poses. Rather, these sheets were clearly intended as records of the picturesque dress of local peasants that could be incorporated into larger compositions of Italian life. Nevertheless, the facility with which Chapman rendered the anatomy, mass, and volume of his sitters is truly impressive, considering that he was probably only twenty years old at the time.

Within two weeks of his arrival in the Eternal City on February 20, 1830, Samuel Finley Breese Morse (1791–1872) began regularly attending the life school of the English Academy. As a founder (in 1826) and current president of the National Academy of Design in New York City, Morse took a keen interest in the prevailing standards of the various national academies—the French, English, Neapolitan, Florentine, and Prussian, to name a few that he mentioned—located in Rome. The illustrious president of the French Academy, the history painter Horace Vernet (1789–1863), cordially received his American counterpart and personally conducted him through his venerable institution's impressive gallery of antique casts. It was, Morse discerned, "a splendid collection selected with great judgment."[14] Although he was already proficient at depicting the human figure, Morse enjoyed communing with his professional fraternity at the English Academy, where he also sharpened his eye to the nuances of different regional costumes in anticipation of an excursion he would make with Chapman that summer to the outlying towns of the Castelli Romani.

Not until 1833 is there another mention of an American studying at the English Academy, in the person of Alfred Jacob Miller (1810–74) of Baltimore. Although he resided with a little-known painter from Virginia, James Macougtry (dates unknown), Miller wrote in his journal that he was the sole American participant from 1833 to 1834.[15] The working arrangements of the English Academy apparently struck the portraitist as novel because he noted:

> Surmounting a platform a pedestal 4 ft. square was placed—on this the model took his position & stood for one hour without scarcely moving a muscle—a large maroon colored curtain fell in graceful folds behind him & a brilliant lamp with a shield 3 ft. in diameter threw a blaze of light over him—bringing the figure out in a wonderful relief.[16]

Miller utilized his brief time in Rome to maximum effect, copying in galleries, painting at the English Academy, and making open-air sketches, including one entitled *Four Monks Overlooking Rome* (fig. 45), executed in the gardens of the Pincian Hill. Already evident is Miller's fluency working in multiple media on one sheet to achieve freshness and vitality—qualities that also characterize his later oeuvre of scenes of the American West.

Within weeks of his arrival in Rome on November 30, 1836—two years after Miller's departure—James Edward Freeman (1808–84), a figure and fancy picture painter from New York, informed a friend at home that "at present I am drawing at the English life school, from fine models 'nude.'"[17] The emphasis placed on the word "nude" suggests the interesting possibility that the male models perhaps wore loincloths or *caches-sexes*. Either way, Freeman's statement is important firsthand proof that American artists were working from disrobed

*Opposite*
Fig. 45. FOUR MONKS OVERLOOKING ROME, ca. 1833–34

Alfred Jacob Miller (1810–1874)
Black ink, pencil, wash, and watercolor on light brown wove paper
7 x 5⅝ in. (17.8 x 14.3 cm)
Private collection

Pincian Hill - Roma

Monks

45

models at the English Academy by the 1830s. Nearly fifty years later, he described his initial experiences as a student there with the nascent sculptor and fellow New Yorker, Thomas Crawford (1813–57), in his second volume of memoirs, *Gatherings from an Artist's Portfolio in Rome*:

> It was in 1837. A half-ruined chapel in the Via dei Maroniti had been converted into a winter evening school for drawing and painting from the nude, and bore the name of the "English Academy." The regulations of the institution permitted two Americans to study there, and at that time these students were Crawford and myself. Crawford had set up his modeling-stand, and Morris Moore, Lauder, "Wee Allan," as we used to call him, Ward (now Royal Academician), and myself had set up our easels to paint standing from Angelo the model, who was placed upon the platform with a large reflecting lamp suspended over his head. In front of us were benches where other students sat with their drawing-boards, copying the model before them, in a weak and feeble way, in charcoal and crayons.[18]

Besides providing fascinating insight into the English Academy's rules, membership, and organization, Freeman's account is noteworthy for naming the "beautiful young Roman," Angelo, from whom they worked.[19] Freeman wrote extensively about the Italian models he encountered during the more than four decades in which he lived abroad, and he took great personal interest in their welfare. He and his Anglo-Italian wife, the amateur sculptor Horatia Augusta

Latilla (1824–97), frequently fed and clothed them, took them into their home, nursed them through sicknesses, and tended them in death.

The English Academy in Rome continued to attract students, but, by 1844, some questioned the merit of a school devoid of proper instruction: "Here are neither books, prints, nor professors," Rippingille complained. "Every English Artist, or would-be artist, is admissible to come, to go, to work, or to play, just as he pleases; and whilst abundant allurements tempt to the wrong, there are no examples tending to the right."[20] A London businessman visiting Rome that same year observed a "schism among the members of the English Academy" following a motion that an "Italian Professor of drawing should be appointed." Those opposed to the idea warned about the "consequences of such a measure":

—the impropriety of introducing an Italian style of drawing to the annihilation of all originality,—the injustice of placing a master over men who never would submit to his criticism, and the un-enviable position in which such a master would necessarily be placed,—the reflection, in fact, upon the state of English art, and other weighty considerations.[21]

Ultimately, the resolution passed—albeit slightly modified. "The master therefore was appointed *not* as Professor of drawing to the English Academy," he reported, "but to give his assistance to such as might ask it."[22] In this way, Tommaso Minardi (1787–1871), a virtuosic draftsman and respected teacher at the Roman Academy of St. Luke, became affiliated with the English Academy in 1845; clearly however, Minardi's allegiance to the cultural movement known as Purism, which looked to the Italian Renaissance as a source of aesthetic inspiration and nationalist pride, caused concern in some quarters.

Although it provided a "spacious and commodious apartment, lighted and warmed, benches, boards, and a living model, to such British subjects . . . as are desirous of studying from the nude," an 1853 article in *Bentley's Miscellany* noted that the English Academy was, nonetheless, virtually empty. "Like so many other benevolently endowed institutions where there is nothing to pay," the contributor remarked, "very few people think it worth their while to go."[23] We do know, however, that some Americans still availed themselves of the life school of the English Academy. Straying from the generally sardonic tone that pervades his published account of his trip to Rome in 1857, the amateur Philadelphia artist Henry Perry Leland (1828–68) sincerely commended the arrangement whereby "with a generosity worthy of all praise, American artists are admitted to the English Academy, with full permission to share with Englishmen the advantages of the life school, free of all cost."[24] Leland also made one significant historical distinction regarding the modeling profession in the Papal States, namely, that the "government prohibiting female models from posing in the nude in the different life schools, it consequently follows that they pose in private studios, as they choose."[25]

Leland informs us that the Virginia-born landscape painter Julius O. de Montalant (1824–78; figs. 7 and 46), who resided in Rome by 1856, attended the English Academy. We also know that two of America's most prominent landscapists, Sanford Robinson Gifford (1823–80) and Albert Bierstadt (1830–1902), frequented it in 1856–57. One of Gifford's sketchbooks contains a small graphite drawing of a full-length male nude (fig. 47) and ten detailed

*Opposite above and above*
Figs. 47 and 48. SKETCHBOOK 1856–57/ITALIAN COSTUMES/ WINDERMERE (TWO SKETCHES), ca. 1857

Sanford Robinson Gifford (1823–1880)
Pencil and watercolor on paper
Sketchbook dimensions:
6 ½ x 9 ¾ in. (16.5 x 24.7 cm)
Albany Institute of History & Art,
Gift of Mrs. William F. Shaw and
Mrs. George G. Cummings, 1966.13.5

*Left*

Fig. 49. COSTUME STUDY OF A
MONK AND A CONTADINA, 1857

Albert Bierstadt (1830–1902)
Oil on paper on board
11 ¾ x 8 ½ in. (29.8 x 21.5 cm)
Private collection

*Opposite above*

Fig. 50. BELVEDERE TORSO,
ca. 1838–41

Samuel Bell Waugh (1814–1885)
Red conté crayon
on cream wove paper
17 ¾ x 12 ⅜ in. (45 x 31.4 cm)
Private collection

*Opposite below*

Fig. 51. MARGUERITE
AT THE WELL, ca. 1858

William Morris Hunt (1824–1879)
Oil on canvas
21 ¼ x 17 ⅜ in. (53.9 x 44.1 cm)
Private collection

graphite and watercolor costume studies, including a pilgrim, a horseman, a
*pifferaro* (fig. 48), and contadinas from Sora, Arpino, Calabria, Albano, and
Alvito, all made at the English Academy. Among his marginalia about fabric
colors (he was reportedly colorblind), Gifford recorded the names of Minacucci
and Stella, two of the most famous models of the era. Leland discussed them
in his inimitably droll manner as well:

> The powers of endurance of the female models were better than
> those of the men; and they would strike a position and keep it for an
> hour, almost immovable. Noticeable among these women was one
> named Minacucci, who, though over seventy years old, had all the
> animation and spirit of one not half her age, and would keep her
> position with the steadiness of a statue. She had, in her younger
> days, been a model for Canova; had outlived two generations; and

was now posing for a third. If you have ever seen many figure paintings executed in Rome, your chance is good to have seen Minacucci's portrait over and over again. . . . The fact is, they do want a new model for the Madonna badly in Rome; for Giacinta is growing old and fat, and Stella, since she married that cobbler, has lost her angelic expression. The small boy who used to pose for angels has smoked himself too yellow, and the man who stood for Charity has gone out of business.[26]

Bierstadt almost certainly painted *Costume Study of a Monk and a Contadina* (fig. 49), in which one figure is superimposed over the other as the artist turned his sheet of prepared paper to use it twice, at the English Academy rather than in the field. The strongly cast shadows that suggest an artificial light source, the wooden staff—a common academy prop for maintaining long poses—that each figure holds, and the incongruous empty shoe that anchors the bottom right corner would seem to corroborate this theory. Like Gifford, Bierstadt specified the origin of each costume, penciling "San Carlino" below the monk and "Chevara," a phonetic spelling of the village of Cervara, next to the contadina.

## Towards an American Academy of Art

By the early 1840s, as more painters and sculptors made the long ocean voyage from the United States to study in Rome, the English Academy's allotment of two seats to them proved inadequate, and interest in establishing a national academy for Americans grew. When he arrived in Rome in 1838 Samuel Bell Waugh (1814–85), an amiable portrait and figure painter from Philadelphia, made drawings of plaster casts, such as his *Belvedere Torso* (fig. 50), at either the English Academy or the French Academy. Such drawings instilled in the novitiate fundamental techniques of delineation and an appreciation for the classical canon of beauty, honing his technical and critical acumen in preparation for working from the living model. The following year, Waugh began a "costume class" in his Roman studio, but he did not limit it to Americans, nor even Anglophones. "Sometimes at our evening parties when we would entertain artists of all nations," Waugh remembered, "there would be heard six or seven different languages."[27]

A clever, quick, and successful painter of grand tour portrait souvenirs, Waugh could afford to hire his own models and, as a result of his extensive peregrinations throughout the peninsula in which he literally purchased the clothes off peasants' backs, he had a ready supply of authentic outfits:

> We particularly enjoyed the costumes which are most interesting and distinctive about here, each town having a particular mode of its own. The coloring is charming and becomes the naturally beautiful women well. I procured several of these costumes, always making a sketch in color of the peasant in the costume I purchased for future reference, otherwise it would have been difficult to recall the many details and so spoil the effect.[28]

While it is tempting to think that the five oil studies by Waugh in this exhibition, *Brigand from Terracina, Two Pifferari, Seated Contadina with Downcast Eyes, Contadina with a Tambourine*, and *Contadina with a Guitar* (figs. 52–56), may be examples of the aides-mémoires he painted in the field, their size, level of finish, even lighting, and shallow settings make it more likely that they were staged in his studio. That we can only see the facial features of one of the men in *Two Pifferrari* may indicate that one model posed twice in different garb.

Buying Italian costumes for future reference was not an uncommon practice. "A whole suit of female dress consisting of half a dozen articles costs about 7 Dollars, much of it made of such stuffs as cannot be found at home," Asher Brown Durand (1796–1886) told his wife. He purchased several garments from

*Below left*

Fig. 52. BRIGAND FROM TERRACINA. ca. 1838–41

Samuel Bell Waugh (1814–1885)
Oil on paper on board
15 ½ x 10 ¾ in. (39.3 x 27.3 cm)
Private collection

models he hired to come to his studio in Rome in 1840–41. "These personages, both male and female," he explained, "make a business of sitting as models for Artists, 3 and 4 hours on a stretch for which they receive 5 pauls, about 50 cents." Additionally, Durand informed her that "part of my evenings, when not working at my room, is employed in drawing at the Life School."[29]

As Durand mentioned, other life schools, besides the national academies, operated in Rome.[30] Because they charged fees, however, they were not a viable option for everyone, especially the landscape painters who could not necessarily justify the expense. A report on one of these commercial enterprises, published in the *Literary World* in 1848, highlighted a few differences, but mostly similarities, between them and the gratis English Academy. "Everything here is arranged expressly for the comfort and convenience of the students," the correspondent began:

> Three ranges of seats of different elevations form a semicircle, and in the center of this amphitheater stands the model, on an elevated platform. There is a large shaded light for the model, and a small one for each student, placed all along on the seats, which are somewhat like little school desks. Back of these seats are raised stands for the students in sculpture. There are persons in attendance

*Above center*

Fig. 53. TWO PIFFERARI. ca. 1838–41

Samuel Bell Waugh (1814–1885)
Oil on paper on board
15 ½ x 11 ½ in. (39.3 x 29.2 cm)
Private collection

*Above right*

Fig. 54. SEATED CONTADINA WITH DOWNCAST EYES. ca. 1838–41

Samuel Bell Waugh (1814–1885)
Oil on paper on board
15 ¼ x 11 ½ in. (38.7 x 29.2 cm)
Private collection

who trim the lights, bring the cups of water, and perform any
other little necessary office, without the students leaving their
seats. The life school begins at dusk and continues two hours, then
commences the costume sitting, which lasts another two hours.
The models stand the whole time without resting. I was surprised
to find persons maintain difficult positions so long, but it is done
to perfection, scarcely a muscle changes; sometimes a very good
model stands longer than required.[31]

The writer's concluding observation that the "old monk who was on the stand at the time of my visit, stood like a statue; had he been of marble he would have been no better" conjures up for us George Loring Brown's (1814–89) watercolor, *Costume Study of an Eminento Monk* (fig. 59). Brown's arrival in Italy coincided with Durand's, and there is reason to believe they attended the same Roman life school.[32]

Throughout his extended sojourn in Italy from 1840 to 1859, Brown regularly patronized life schools and noted in his account book for 1856 that the fee for one month was eleven scudi, roughly equivalent to eleven dollars. Compare this to the fifteen scudi he paid monthly for rooms he shared with the American neoclassical sculptor Randolph Rogers (1825–92), the ten scudi for his studio, or the twenty-five scudi that a hand-carved and gilded Italian frame cost, and we can easily grasp that the concept of a national academy funded through public subscription possessed enormous appeal. Not that Brown was destitute; on the contrary, he was a fully mature, highly successful artist who earned anywhere from 150 to 300 scudi per painting, depending on the size. Taken together with the drawings, watercolors, and oil sketches that he made in nature (figs. 58, 108, and 109), Brown's life studies constituted the building blocks of his large finished canvases of idyllic Italian landscapes. Compositions with the monumental dimensions of *Effect near Noon—along the Appian Way* (fig. 39), for instance, benefit tremendously from the introduction of staffage figures to indicate scale and depth, alleviate the monotony of verdant foliage, and lead the viewer into the narrative.

*Above*
Fig. 57. PORTRAIT OF BERTEL THORVALDSEN, 1838
Samuel Bell Waugh (1814–1885)
Oil on canvas on board
29 x 24 in. (73.6 x 60.9 cm)
Private collection

# The American Academy

While American artists perceived a need for their own national academy in Rome, they could not convince any of their countrymen to endow one—that is, until 1842. "An American Academy has been started here and is at present going on well. A good room is provided with models every evening," Thomas Cole (1801–48) wrote to Durand from Rome in March 1842.[33] The Boston painter Abel Nichols (1815–60) noted that summer that "we have just established an American Academy in Rome; there are to be lectures and every evening some portion of a body is to be dissected to paint from: also two hours each day we paint from the 'Modello Nudo.'"[34] Thomas Pritchard Rossiter (1818–71) elaborated on the American Academy's genesis in a letter to the painter John Frederick Kensett (1816–72), whom he and Cole had just left in Paris:

> A number of gentlemen here contributed a very handsome sum for the founding of an academy for American students. Upon their return home they have in a measure promised to raise 8 or 10 thousand dollars for purchasing a large building—then a sum for a library, gallery of casts, and a number of professors with a life school. All this to the student will be gratuitous and of course very cozy.[35]

Assuring Kensett that "there is a prospect hereafter that to Americans every facility will be afforded for their advancement," Rossiter explained that, until the funding for permanent quarters could be secured, their benefactors—none identified by name—had already "fitted up a room for a life academy where the American artists (at present numbering 11) meet every night and work away like a pack of fellows intent on individual and national glory."[36] With Thomas Crawford serving as president, the American consul George Washington Greene (1811–83) as secretary, and Thomas Cole and Luther Terry (1813–1900) forming a committee, the other members of the nascent American Academy were Freeman, William Brown Cooper (1811–1900), James De Veaux (1812–44), Louis Lang (1814–93), David Hunter Strother (1816–88), Frederick Fink (1817–49), and Theodore M. V. Kennedy (d. 1849). The following January Rossiter apprised Kensett that "our Academy is in full operation and every thing goes on harmoniously. Every night we meet for two hours numbering seven members."[37]

In a significant development, the American Academy hired an Italian drawing master named Giovanni Francesco Ferrero (dates unknown) for the 1842–43 and 1843–44 seasons. Ferrero was a noted anatomist and published a book of engravings of the Vatican sculpture collection; he would also teach the American neoclassical sculptor Edward Sheffield Bartholomew (1822–58) in the 1850s. Unlike the dissent that greeted Minardi at the English Academy, Rossiter reported unanimous approval of Ferrero's instruction: "As we have a capital professor we all flatter ourselves we are improving rapidly."[38] Seth Wells Cheney (1810–56), a respected engraver and draftsman who had studied in the Parisian ateliers of Paul Delaroche (1797–1856) and Eugène Isabey (1803–86) in the 1830s, revealed that, under Ferrero, "I find I must make a school-boy of myself again."[39] Years later, Cheney's wife and biographer discussed the enduring impact that Ferrero had on his students during the winter of 1843–44:

> This was the last year of [the American Academy's] existence, but our artists profited well by it. The teacher was Ferrero, and his clear, exact lessons were always remembered by Seth with great gratitude. He laid great stress upon exactness and delicacy of line, often revealing to them the nice expression of slight variations in the form. He also laid great stress on the focusing of light and shadows so that the effect should be clear. Seth often recalled the "troppo confuso," which was the old man's most frequent criticism of his work, and he would often say, "Every shadow has its darkest point, every light its brightest." Ferrero was a fine anatomist, and his plate illustrating the anatomy and proportions of the human figure was Seth's constant study to the end of his life.[40]

The attrition at the American Academy continued so that, by April 1843, the ranks had dwindled to five, and its future was questioned. "Two weeks more will witness its demise," Rossiter noted, "and I query if another national institution will ever be attempted in Rome again."[41] Classes did reconvene that fall, but it would be the last for this first American Academy in Rome because the financial support promised by their anonymous patrons ceased. Thus, we can only speculate on what its long-term effect might have been on the development of American figural art had it been nurtured beyond its infancy to include a life school, curriculum, casts, and a library.

*Above*
Fig. 60. THE SERENADE, 1853
John Gadsby Chapman (1808–1889)
Oil on canvas
17 x 13 in. (43.2 x 33 cm)
Private collection

# The American Sketch Club

*Below*

Fig. 61. SKETCH CLUB
OF AMERICAN ARTISTS
AT ROME, April 26, 1845

Philibert Perraud
(b. 1815)
Daguerreotype, mounted
on cardboard
3.1 x 4.3 in. (8 x 11 cm)
Courtesy of the Miscellaneous
Photograph Collection,
Archives of American Art,
Smithsonian Institution

The void left by the premature demise of the American Academy in 1844 was partially filled when its members reconstituted themselves into the American Sketch Club. It began casually, Daniel Huntington (1816–1906) wrote in late 1843, with informal gatherings in private homes. By the following season, however, it had coalesced, according to the wife of the sculptor Henry Kirke Brown (1814–86):

> Last evening we had the first meeting of the American Sketch Club which will meet every Tuesday evening at the rooms of some one of the members alternately—next Tuesday here. Mrs. Huntington and myself being the only ladies and honorary members will go only to each other's house. There are twelve Amer[ican] artist members which I think are all there are in Rome.[42]

In addition to Huntington and Henry K. Brown, an 1845 group portrait (fig. 61), taken by the pioneering French dageurreotypist Philibert Perraud (b. 1815) identifies Freeman, Terry, Lang, Emanuel Leutze (1816–68), Trevor McClurg (1816–93), Rossiter, George Champlin Mason (1820–94), George Augustus Baker Jr. (1821–80), William Morris Hunt (1824–79), William Henry Powell (1824–79), Nathan F. Baker (1825–91), William B. Chambers (active 1834–57), and Alfred Bujac (dates unknown) as the constituents of the American Sketch Club. Everyone involved thus specialized in depictions of the human figure, be they portraits, fancy pictures, history paintings, genre, or sculpture. While these men possibly pooled their money to hire living models for their evenings together, they certainly were not working from the nude—at least not when the Mmes. Huntington and Brown were present. It seems more probable, from a financial standpoint, that they worked from wooden manikins, lay figures, and *écorché* models or even traded modeling duties among themselves.

Ferrero continued to consult his former students from the American Academy and critiqued the anatomy drawings made by Cheney and his studio partner, the Bostonian Alpheus Carey Morse (1818–93), three times a week. "I have caught the anatomy fever, too," Huntington confessed, "and am trying to gain some knowledge of the joints and muscles."[43] Two graphite sketches by Huntington, *Roman Model in Contadina Dress* and *Costume Sitting for an Evangelist* (figs. 62–63), the first executed in Cheney and Morse's studio in 1843 and the second in Freeman's studio in 1845, give some indication of the variety of subjects his peers were treating on their own. Precisely when and why the American Sketch Club terminated their activities is unknown, but it was almost certainly defunct by 1848, at which time the wealthy amateur Charles Callahan Perkins (1823–86) hosted an intimate group of five—Freeman, Terry, Christopher Pearse Cranch (1813–92), Thomas Hicks (1823–90), and William Wetmore Story (1819–95)—for an evening academy drawing from a nude model at his home.

Surrounded by Rome's abundance of classical statuary of deities and imperial personages, Christian narrative and devotional paintings, and the neoclassical productions of their contemporary international milieu, the Americans were stimulated to improve their understanding of the human form and did not limit

*Above*

Fig. 62. ROMAN MODEL
IN CONTADINA DRESS, 1843
(not in exhibition)

Daniel Huntington (1816–1906)
Dated and inscribed lower right:
"Cheney & Morse's Studio / Rome
Nov 25 / /43"
Graphite on off-white wove paper
7 x 4 ½ in. (17.8 x 11.3 cm)
Private collection

*Left*

Fig. 63. COSTUME SITTING
FOR AN EVANGELIST, 1845
(not in exhibition)

Daniel Huntington (1816–1906)
Inscribed and dated lower right:
"On calling / at Freeman's Studio /
Rome March / 45"
Graphite on off-white wove paper
5 ½ x 8 ½ in. (14 x 21.6 cm)
Private collection

themselves to merely superficial representations of picturesque costumes.
*Salvator Rosa among the Brigands* (fig. 64), the masterpiece of William Henry
Powell's two-and-a-half-year Italian sojourn, manifests the ambitious young history painter's commitment to the technical standards and narrative interests
that prevailed in Rome in the 1840s. Profiting from the city's unsurpassed re-
sources for the artist, Powell synthesized his study of anatomy, period costumes
and props, perspective, and composition to create a work that rivals similar
examples of historical genre of the lives of eminent artists by Europeans and
Americans alike.[44]

*Above*

Fig. 64. SALVATOR ROSA AMONG
THE BRIGANDS, 1846

William Henry Powell (1823–1879)
Oil on canvas
31¾ x 39½ in. (80.6 x 100.3 cm)
Private collection

# Gigi's Academy

"The first facts which strike you in reference to Gigi's academy," according to the same 1853 article from *Bentley's Miscellany* that reported the nearly deserted state of the English Academy, "are that it is intensely hot, crowded, and full of tobacco-smoke."[45] This account is significant because it confirms that the popular for-profit academy run by Luigi Talarici (dates unknown), nicknamed Gigi, in the Via Margutta was operational at a much earlier date than is usually acknowledged. Capturing something of Gigi's unique bohemian atmosphere, Henry Leland encouraged the "traveler in search of the picturesque by all means to visit it, particularly if it is in the same location it was" in the 1850s:

> It was over a stable, in the second story of a tumbledown old house, frequented by dogs, cats, fleas, and rats; in a room say fifty feet long by twenty wide. A semicircle of desks and wooden benches went round the platform, where stood the male models nude, or, on other evenings, male and female models in costumes, Roman or Neapolitan. Oil lamps gave enough light to enable the artists who generally attended there to draw, and color, in oils or water colors, the costumes.[46]

Leland numbered "Americans, Danes, Germans, Spaniards, French, Italians, English, and Russians" among the students, and, occasionally, "a sedate-looking Englishwoman or two would come in quietly, make a sketch, and go away un-molested, and almost unnoticed."[47] The author of the 1876 chronicle, *English Female Artists*, corroborated that although the English Academy in Rome did not allow females into their life classes, Gigi's, which she noted was "free and republican in its internal arrangements," did. "No lady need have the least hesi-tation in taking her place," she assured her readers. "She will meet with nothing but kindness and courtesy—for all Italians are born gentlemen."[48]

Evenings at Gigi's began with a nude subject that lasted two hours. When the writer for *Bentley's Miscellany* attended, the model appeared on a rough-hewn wooden cross, his "wrists lashed with cord to its upper member":

> A strong light from two reflecting lamps, hung above his head, bring out all the unfortunate victim's strained and starting muscles in bold relief. The expression of the face indicates a good deal of physical suffering and weariness, which is not to be wondered at, considering that he is now near the end of his second hour.[49]

The author reflected at length that, for a Protestant, there was something "startling" in "this sort of gross real life representation," especially when one contemplated the "base" model—"a handsome deity, sensual-featured lazzaron [slacker], very tired of being crucified at seven-pence an hour." Nevertheless, the writer granted that in "Catholic countries, where there is a great demand for pictures of the crucifixion, artists must learn to paint it, and this is the way." Indeed, it was emphasized that the "artists do the face last, that they may gather some useful hints for the expression of bodily suffering."[50]

"The students of the *nude* are gone," the article continued, "and the costume students have taken possession of the horse-shoe tiers of drawing-desks." The proposed subject was Velasquez at his easel, dressed in a "slashed doublet of orange satin, with crimson silk hose of wonderful length, and a pair of bunched-up sky-blue damask inexpressibles, of equally wonderful shortness." A vociferous discussion about Velasquez's stance ensued, with the "harsh gutturals" of the German tongue predominant, until finally the work began:

> In some, bold and dashing effects come out with every touch of the brush; others linger in the penciled outline, gaining a smudgy correctness under much india-rubber; some remain hopelessly meager and spiritless to the end. Some few of the students do their sketch in oils, but the great majority in water-colours. There were not above three or four out of all the fifty or sixty, whose drawings showed any great talent or promise.[51]

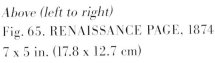

*Above (left to right)*
Fig. 65. RENAISSANCE PAGE, 1874
7 x 5 in. (17.8 x 12.7 cm)

Fig. 66. LADY IN ROCOCO
DRESS, ca. 1874
7 x 5 in. (17.8 x 12.7 cm)

Fig. 67. MAN IN
GREEN DOUBLET AND
RED HOSE, ca. 1874
7 x 5 in. (17.8 x 12.7 cm)

Conrad Wise Chapman (1842–1910)
Oil on card on board
Private collection

Three small oil sketches by Conrad Wise Chapman (1842–1910), *Renaissance Page*, *Lady in Rococo Dress*, and *Man in Green Doublet and Red Hose* (figs. 65–67), are archetypal examples of this kind of academy work, characterized by dramatic lighting, uncomplicated poses, vivid colors, textural effects, and shallow backgrounds. Conrad and his brother John Linton (1839–1905), known as Jack to distinguish him from their father and teacher John Gadsby Chapman, undoubtedly frequented Gigi's Academy, which was located just one street away from the family home at Via del Babuino 135.

Conrad Chapman kept the three aforementioned period costume studies in his possession throughout his life and referred to them for the decorative *fêtes gallantes* he would paint in Mexico in the 1880s and 1890s. Similarly, he retained at least two other groupings of costume studies in oil, all probably executed in a Roman academy. The first, consisting of *Father and Daughter Begging*, *Bagpiper (Zampognaro)*, *Young Contadino*, and *Woman from the Abruzzi* (figs. 68–71), depicts peasant types that are easily differentiated by their age, gender, or attribute posed against monochrome backgrounds; whereas the second, comprised of *Woman of Albano*, *Study of "Autumn" for "The Four Seasons,"* *Woman of Sorrento*, and *Woman of Ciociaria* (figs. 72–75), is concerned with the subtleties of dress that distinguished various regions and is

*Above (left to right)*
Fig. 68. FATHER AND
DAUGHTER BEGGING, ca. 1860
7 x 5 in. (17.8 x 12.7 cm)

Fig. 69. BAGPIPER
(ZAMPOGNARO), 1860
7 x 5 in. (17.8 x 12.7 cm)

Fig. 70. YOUNG CONTADINO, 1861
7 x 5 in. (17.8 x 12.7 cm)

Conrad Wise Chapman (1842–1910)
Oil on card on board
Private collection

finished with representative landscapes. In assembling this corpus of studies, Conrad Chapman could assure his international clientele of grand tourists that his studio scenes of Italy were populated with suitably attired figures.

Their diminutive size notwithstanding, the amount of detail, level of finish, and characterization that Conrad Chapman attained in his academy studies merit particular notice since, according to Leland, the "model only posed about two hours," and the "artists had to work very fast to get even a rough sketch finished in that short time." That said, he did perceive that when the model took a break at the end of the first hour "these minutes were seldom wasted by the artist, who improved them to finish the lines of his drawing or dash in color."[52] Another visitor to Gigi's, extensively quoted by Augustus J. C. Hare (1834–1903) in his 1876 travel guide, *Walks in Rome*, explained it differently:

> Every evening the subject for the next night is chalked up on a black board beside the platform—for the next *two* nights rather; for each model poses for two evenings; the position of his feet being chalked upon the platform, so as to secure the same attitude on the second evening. Consequently, four hours are allowed for each drawing.[53]

This same author related that the "costumes are regulated by Church time and seasons. During Lent the models wear medieval dress; during the winter and carnival, Italian costumes of the present day; and with Easter begin mere draperies, *pieghe*, or folds, as they are technically called." Moreover, each drapery study lasted only one evening "as it would be impossible to secure the same folds twice over."[54] Might George Whitefield Hatch's (1806–67) brush and ink wash sketch of a *Woman in Classical Dress* (fig. 77), the singular example of a female wearing a Greek chiton in a sketchbook from his 1841 Italian tour, constitute just such an academy exercise?

Gigi's Academy flourished throughout the 1860s while, ironically, the English Academy floundered. The writer for *Bentley's Miscellany* conjectured that Gigi, himself a former model who had earned the moniker of Hercules, took "more pains to procure attractive models than the honorary managers" of the English

*Opposite bottom*
Fig. 71. WOMAN FROM
THE ABRUZZI, ca. 1861
Conrad Wise Chapman (1842–1910)
Oil on card on board
7 x 5 in. (17.8 x 12.7 cm)
Private collection

*Right and below (left to right)*
Fig. 72. WOMAN OF ALBANO, 1874
7 x 5 in. (17.8 x 12.7 cm)

Fig. 73. STUDY OF "AUTUMN" FOR
"THE FOUR SEASONS," ca. 1867
7 x 5 in. (17.8 x 12.7 cm)

Fig. 74. WOMAN OF
SORRENTO, 1874
7 x 5 in. (17.8 x 12.7 cm)

Fig. 75. WOMAN OF
CIOCIARIA, ca. 1868
7 x 5 in. (17.8 x 12.7 cm)

Conrad Wise Chapman (1842–1910)
Oil on card on board
Private collection

Academy.[55] Upon arriving in Rome in October 1869 to assume the post of U.S. consul to the Papal States, the New York painter David Maitland Armstrong (1836–1918) patronized Gigi's Academy with his compatriot, Frederic Crowninshield (1845–1918), who would become director in 1911 of an entirely new entity, the American Academy in Rome (established in 1894). In his memoirs, *Day before Yesterday*, Armstrong recalled of the proprietor that "I never knew his surname—but all he did was to exact his fee each month and provide good light, heat, and a model, and also—for two soldi—large hunks of coarse bread, called *mollica*, for rubbing out marks."[56] More significant still was Armstrong's assertion that the model "was sometimes a young woman clothed only in a mask, or sometimes without it; sometimes a naked Arab, or a peasant boy."[57] Unfortunately, Armstrong did not state the specific year in which females began to disrobe in Rome's public academies, but we may postulate that this breakthrough perhaps occurred only after the pope forfeited temporal rule over the city in 1870.

*Above*
Fig. 76. MONK FROM MONTE CAVI, 1841
George Whitefield Hatch (1805–1867). Brush and ink wash on buff wove paper in bound sketchbook
Sketchbook dimensions: 3 7/16 x 5 3/16 in. (8.7 x 13.1 cm)
Private collection

*Above*
Fig. 77. WOMAN IN CLASSICAL DRESS, 1841
George Whitefield Hatch (1805–1867)
Brush and ink wash on buff wove paper in bound sketchbook
Sketchbook dimensions: 4 x 5 5/8 in. (10.1 x 14.3 cm)
Private collection

# The Models

"Professional models in Rome may be divided into two classes—those who sit or stand in costume, and those who are models for the nude. The first are mostly employed by the painters, and the last by the sculptors," Freeman stipulated in his memoirs. "There is nothing in painting or sculpture," he observed, "where bones, muscle, color, and costumes are wanted, for which a model may not be found in Rome."[58] Each winter peasants from outlying regions would congregate on the Spanish Steps, the rendezvous point for artists and models—or, as William Gardiner (1770–1853) called it, a "market of physiognomy"—to seek employment in Rome's academies, life schools, and studios.[59] Sarah Jane Lippincott (1803–1904), who wrote under the name Grace Greenwood, delighted in the "very amusing and skillful piece of canvassing" that occurred there:

> These various candidates for artistic favor seem to have the most social and agreeable relations with each other—indeed, I have remarked the patriarch chatting and laughing with the brigand in a familiar manner, scarcely in keeping with his own venerable character. But, let an artist or two ascend the steps, and, presto! the dark-eyed young girls cease their idle gossip and spring into position—look archly or mournfully over the left shoulder, or with clasped hands modestly contemplate the pavement—the pretty peasant woman snatches up the baby she had left to creep about at its own sweet will, and bends over it tender and Madonna-like, while, at a word from her, a skin-clad little shepherd boy drops his game of pitch penny, and takes up his *rôle* of St. John. Perhaps a dark, dignified, but somewhat rheumatic old woman, with her head wrapped up in a brown cloth, makes a modest venture of herself as St. Anna, while the fine old man I have described makes the most of the comparatively unimportant character of St. Joseph, or, separating himself entirely from the group, looks authoritative as Moses, or inspired as Isaiah, or resolute as Peter. The handsome bravo or brigand gives a fiercer twist to his mustache, slouches his pointed black hat, appears to be concealing a dagger under his brown cloak, or on the point of drawing an imaginary pistol from his belt, sets his teeth, scowls, and cultivates the diabolical generally in attitude and expression.[60]

Greenwood's amusing account of the machinations of the motley assemblage on the Spanish Steps aside, modeling was, ultimately, a job. Gardiner, one of the few memoirists of the period to consider the model's point of view, reflected on the feelings of the "handsome female, in a rich rose-coloured satin dress" who posed for an hour and a half at a public costume school one evening. "What was the predominant feeling of this girl on seeing the thirty-three delineations of herself? Was she flattered by being chosen for her beauty?" he wondered. "Probably not. More likely it was the money alone that repaid her for the penance she had endured." Writing as a spectator, not an artist, Gardiner wrote, "I felt for her situation, and left before she quitted the table."[61]

One denizen of the Spanish Steps who, although not a professional model, attracted enormous interest in his physiognomy was Beppo.[62] He unwittingly gained international fame in 1835 when Hans Christian Andersen (1805–75) made him a character in his popular novel, *The Improvisatore*:

*Below*
Fig. 79. DAUGHTER OF THE VINE (STUDY FOR "RUBÁIYÁT"), ca. 1881–83

Elihu Vedder (1836–1923)
Black and white chalk
on light brown wove paper
11 x 12 in. (27.9 x 30.4 cm)
Private collection

Born with two withered legs which lay crossed under him, he had
from his earliest childhood an extraordinary facility in moving himself forwards with his hands. These he stuck under a frame which
was fastened at both ends to a board, and by help of this he could
move himself forward almost as easily as any other person with
healthy and strong feet. He sat daily, as has been said, upon the
Spanish Steps, never indeed begging, but exclaiming, with a crafty
smile, to every passer-by, *"buon giorno!"* and that even after the
sun was gone down.[63]

Beppo earned the moniker, "the King of the Beggars," for his haughty manner,
the esteem with which other beggars regarded him, as well as his evident suc-
cess in soliciting money—he was, Nathaniel Hawthorne (1804–64) declared,

"the millionaire of his ragged fraternity." In 1860, he commented in *The Marble Faun* that "it is a wonder that no artist paints him as the cripple whom Saint Peter heals."[64] It is interesting, therefore, that when Conrad Chapman captured Beppo's likeness in a painting entitled *Beppo, King of the Beggars* (unlocated) the following year, he portrayed him in contemporary dress, straightforward, and unromanticized. John Gadsby Chapman made an engraving after it (fig. 81), which demonstrates that the young artist did not exploit his subject's deformities, but focused on his penetrating gaze and robust physicality. Beppo was as much a fixture of Rome as were the aqueducts, the Forum, or the Belvedere Torso at the Vatican, to which the sculptor William W. Story compared him in his 1864 chronicle, *Roba di Roma*. When the landscapist and Transcendentalist poet Christopher Pearse Cranch encountered Beppo in 1858 after a ten-year absence from the Eternal City, he admitted, "I deliberately stopped, opened my purse, took out a heavy two *baiocco* piece and dropped it in his hat,—for the sake of old times. . . . I could as little have missed old Beppo in Rome, and on his place, as I could have missed the boat fountain at the bottom of the Spanish Stairs."[65]

One of the more popular models in Rome in the middle decades of the century was Michele, who apprised Freeman that "most of the painters want me for old shepherds, leaning on a long staff, watching sheep, with a dog at my feet.

*Below*
Fig. 82. DOLCE FAR NIENTE, 1850
Thomas Hicks (1823–1890)
Oil on canvas
20 ½ x 29 ⅜ in. (52.1 x 74.6 cm)
Private collection

I feel that my back is beginning to get crooked by bending so much to represent venerable people, and I am not forty-five yet." Michele offered his unique perspective as a model for paintings, like John Gadsby Chapman's *Shepherd of the Campagna* (fig. 80), in which, Michele complained, "I have to stand without moving a limb for two hours. *Per Bacco!* I often envy the dog. Every muscle has ached to that degree that I have sworn inwardly (*accidente*) enough to sink a ship."[66] In stark contrast to Michele's exertions was that of Thomas Hicks' fortunate model for *Dolce Far Niente* (fig. 82), immortalized in a recumbent position reminiscent of the famed grand tour portrait of Goethe by Wilhelm Tischbein (1786, Städelsches Museum, Frankfurt am Main). "Uneducated as he was, and a mountaineer, Michele was a man of considerable refinement," Freeman wrote.[67] "There was in his bearing and peasant's dress a care and nicety which showed a higher cultivation than belonged to most of the *cioceari*":

> His *cioce*, or moccasins, as we would call them, were better made, and the white stockings bound in cleaner bands or strips of leather; his breeches of finer material and deeper blue. His waistband was more ample, and of the richest red; his *guardia macchia*, or sheepskin coat, of finer wool. His sack, made of a fox's skin, pending from his shoulders, had an air of elegance, and his pointed hat, with a modest plume, was in harmony with the lank, black hair which fell to his shoulders. The large, coarse cloak, with its formal cape, fell over his straight, strong figure with a certain air and dignity which one often observes among this class of *contadini*.[68]

Not infrequently multiple generations of one family entered the modeling business, and Michele launched his daughter Giovannina's career when she was only four years old. "There were few days that this little creature did not earn five francs for her father," Freeman marveled.[69]

Summer witnessed the exodus of both artists and models from Rome to the surrounding hill towns of the Castelli Romani, the former seeking to escape the heat and threat of malaria and the latter returning to their lives of manual labor in the fields and villages. As a result, the artists now had to seek out peasants with the look they wanted and coax them into posing. Freeman characteristically recounted one occasion in Ariccia, where he spent several summers in the late 1840s and early 1850s, when he exercised tremendous tact and perseverance to secure his desired model:

I walked about the village, seeing upon many broken doorsteps subjects for my pencil. . . . I came upon a ruined doorway, surpassing all the others in picturesque untidiness. On the doorsill sat the venerable *nonna* whirling the spool of flaxen thread with her right hand; with her left, from the distaff she pulled the unspun material to feed the twisting process. A grade beneath, her daughter nursed a sickly infant on her lap; still below, *her* children, of various ages, with scant, torn costumes, laughed, romped, and screeched. One of these was a lovely girl with golden hair and light blue eyes (that rare peculiarity seen in Southern Italy). . . . She was a wild, uncombed little beauty, and I made up my mind at once that I must paint her. I told the thin, starved-faced mother so, and the haggard-looking grandmother as well, but both shook their heads and said: "It is thought a bad sign among us *contadini* to have our pictures painted. There is a belief that death follows soon after." It was not the first time I had encountered this superstition and had vanquished it; the offer of one paul an hour conquered it now, and pretty Checca was to be my model.[70]

The serendipity involved in finding a muse struck Freeman for its poignancy, and he commemorated the experience not only in his memoirs but in a painting as well, *Costume Picture* (fig. 91). In this masterful composition, Freeman portrays a painter (curiously not a self-portrait) inspired to creative action by Checca's exotic appearance and innate grace, while he is, in fact, surrounded by a multitude of picturesque subjects suitable for his canvas. He could just as easily paint the impish brother and bashful sister standing next to him, the contadino sulking in the corner, the weatherworn crone and her beautiful daughter supporting a swaddled infant, or, to his right, the trio of rustic maidens taking their goods to market. *Costume Picture* captures the quintessence of working from the living model—the choices made, the shortcomings overlooked, the romantic aura that colors the artist's perception.

One nineteenth-century commentator wrote that Rome's academies and costume schools functioned as the "great manufactory of those *contadinas*, who, on canvas or paper, appear to have been limned at Tivoli, Grotta Ferrata, or Frascati, reposing in vine-garlanded bowers, or on picturesque balconies."[71] Their seminal importance to the community of artists waned, however, as photographs of both clothed and unclothed figures (figs. 87–90) were increasingly employed in the studios, and the perceived need of working from life diminished. Ironically, photography also adversely affected the market for Italian-themed genre paintings, fancy pictures, and landscape paintings as grand tourists and armchair travelers purchased the same affordable, portable, and arguably more accurate photographs as the artists did. The audience for images of Italian people nonetheless persisted, even if the preferred medium changed. In the twenty-first century our appreciation of the aesthetic qualities of these paintings, sculptures, and photographs is, in many instances, accompanied by a complementary interest in them as historical documents of a bygone era, a situation that Freeman foretold when he mused that the "lineaments of our Abruzzi models will be known to as distant a future as linen and paint will endure. I cannot but think it a species of immortality for the models, this having their features and forms handed down to future generations."[72]

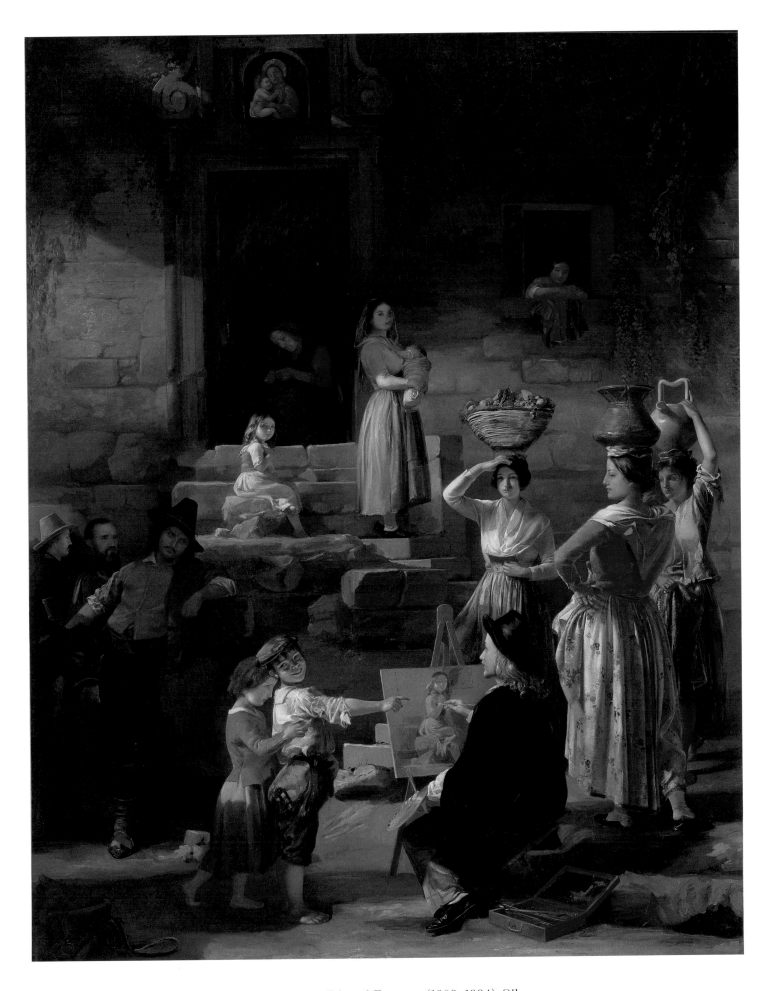

*Above:* Fig. 91. COSTUME PICTURE, 1857. James Edward Freeman (1808–1884). Oil on canvas
59³/₁₆ x 45 ½ in. (150.3 x 115.5 cm). Private collection

# Notes

1. Henry T. Tuckerman, *Book of the Artists: American Artist Life* (New York: G. P. Putnam and Son, 1867), 25. All spelling has been standardized and corrected.

2. Barbara Novak, "Arcady Revisited," in Charles Eldredge, *The Arcadian Landscape: Nineteenth-Century American Painters in Italy* (Lawrence, Kansas: University of Kansas Museum of Art, 1972), xvii.

3. Christine A. Dupont writes that nineteenth-century artists made no distinction between the art of Italy and its modern people, and she cites one occasion when Pierre-Narcisse Guérin (1774–1833) asked his student Léon Coignet (1794–1880) who bore the mark of Italy more greatly, the works of art or the "physiognomy of the people." See Christine A. Dupont, *Modèles italiens et traditions nationales: Les artistes belges en Italie (1830–1914)* 2 vols. (Brussels and Rome: Institut Historique Belge de Rome, 2005), 1:556.

4. Irene Weir, *Robert W. Weir, Artist* (New York: House of Field-Doubleday, 1947), 19.

5. "Origin of the English Academy. [From a copy of the Circular, printed at Rome, with which we have been favoured.]." *London Literary Gazette* no. 322 (March 22, 1823): 188.

6. C., "Fine Arts. English Academy at Rome." *London Literary Gazette* no. 320 (March 8, 1823): 155.

7. C., "Fine Arts. Anglo-Roman School." *London Literary Gazette* no. 329 (May 10, 1823): 298.

8. "Origin," *Gazette*, 188.

9. [Edward Villiers Rippingille], "An Evening's Gossip with a Painter. Palette and Chatworthy in Conversation." *Artist and Amateur's Magazine* (February 1844): 356.

10. The early history and movements of the English Academy are difficult to reconstruct, especially as their archives went missing in 1940. See Holger Hoock, *The King's Artists: The Royal Academy of Arts and the Politics of British Culture, 1760–1840* (New York: Oxford University Press, Inc., 2003), 122n70.

11. Weir, *Weir*, 20.

12. Joseph Pearson Farley, *Three Rivers: The James, the Potomac, the Hudson. A Retrospect of Peace and War* (New York and Washington: The Neale Publishing Company, 1910), 266.

13. Ibid., 267.

14. Samuel F. B. Morse, Diary, March 29, 1830. Reel 32, Samuel F. B. Morse Papers, Manuscript Division, Library of Congress, Washington, DC.

15. Little is known about Macougtry, who appears to have only been active from 1828–34. He is almost certainly the "Macontra" listed in E. P. Richardson and Otto Wittmann Jr.'s *Travelers in Arcadia: American Artists in Italy, 1830–1875* (Detroit: Detroit Institute of Arts, 1951), 66.

16. Page 39 of Miller's Journal, as quoted in Karen Dewees Reynolds and others, *Alfred Jacob Miller: Artist on the Oregon Trail* (Fort Worth: Amon Carter Museum, 1982), cat. no. 2. This catalogue entry reproduces Miller's *Study in the Life School, Rome* (1834, oil on paper on board, Private collection), a portrait bust of a male model.

17. James E. Freeman to Henry W. Bellows, December 1, 1836, Henry W. Bellows Papers, Massachusetts Historical Society.

18. James E. Freeman, *Gatherings from an Artist's Portfolio in Rome* (Boston: Roberts Brothers, 1883), 287. In the original text the Via dei Maroniti is misidentified as "Via Marianetti," undoubtedly a translation error by Freeman's American editors. The other artists mentioned are the English painter Morris Moore (1811–85), one of two Scottish brothers James Eckford Lauder (1811–69) or Robert Scott Lauder (1803–69), Patrick Allan (1813–90, later called Patrick Allan-Fraser), and the English painter Edward Matthew Ward (1817–79).

19. Ibid., 288.

20. [Rippingille], "Gossip," 356.

21. Samuel Bevan, *Sand and Canvas; A Narrative of Adventures in Egypt, with a Sojourn among the Artists in Rome* (London: Charles Gilpin, 1849), 339.

22. Ibid.

23. "A Journey from Westminster Abbey to St. Peter's," *Bentley's Miscellany* 34 (1853): 512.

24. Henry P. Leland, *Americans in Rome* (New York: Charles T. Evans, 1863), 105. Leland's account was first serialized in the *Continental Monthly* as "Maccaroni and Canvas."

25. Ibid.

26. Ibid., 106–07.

27. Samuel Bell Waugh, typescript of Journal, 47–48. Waugh Family Papers, 1838–1971. Archives of American Art, Smithsonian Institution.

28. Ibid., 25.

29. Asher B. Durand to Mrs. Asher B. (Mary) Durand, January 15, 1841. Asher B. Durand Papers, Manuscripts and Archives Division, The New York Public Library, Astor, Lenox and Tilden Foundations. Durand did not specify which life school he attended.

30. The for-profit life schools in Rome during this period are not well-documented, perhaps because their locations were impermanent, and knowledge of them was disseminated by word of mouth in order for the proprietor to avoid regulation and taxes.

31. "Foreign Correspondence," *Literary World* 2, no. 52 (January 29, 1848): 631.

32. Durand's traveling companion, John William Casilear (1811–93), painted a virtually identical monk, signed and dated lower right: "Rome JWC / 1841" (Princeton University Art Museum).

33. Thomas Cole to Asher B. Durand, March 8, 1842. Thomas Cole Papers, 1821–1863. New York State Library, Albany, New York.

34. Mary Eliot Nichols, "Abel Nichols, Artist," *Historical Collections of the Danvers Historical Society* 29 (1941): 22.

35. Thomas P. Rossiter to John F. Kensett, February 2, 1842. John F. Kensett Papers, 1832–1872. New York State Library.

36. Ibid.

37. Ibid., January 8, 1843.

38. Ibid.

39. Ednah D. Cheney, *Memoir of Seth W. Cheney, Artist* (Boston: Lee and Shepard Publishers, 1881), 80.

40. Ibid., 75–78. The author incorrectly states his name as Giorgio Ferrero.

41. Thomas P. Rossiter to Thomas Cole, April 23, 1843. Cole Papers.

42. Lydia Brown to Mrs. Owen (Adoline) Taft, November 27, 1844. Henry Kirke Brown Papers, 1836–1893. Manuscript Division, Library of Congress.

43. Daniel Huntington to Cornelius Ver Bryck, December 5, 1843. Huntington Family Papers, 1792–1901. Owned by Channing M. Huntington II; micro-filmed by the Archives of American Art, Smithsonian Institution.

44. For more on the subject, see Bernard Barryte, "History and Legend in T. J. Barker's *The Studio of Salvator Rosa in the Mountains of the Abruzzi, 1865*," *The Art Bulletin* 71, no. 4 (December 1989): 660–73; and Francis Haskell, "The Old Masters in Nineteenth-Century Painting," in *Past and Present in Art and Taste: Selected Essays* (New Haven: Yale University Press, 1987), 90–115.

45. "Journey," *Bentley's*, 514.

46. Leland, *Americans*, 105–06.

47. Ibid., 106.

48. Ellen C. Clayton, *English Female Artists* 2 vols. (London: Tinsley Brothers, 1876), 160–61.

49. "Journey," *Bentley's*, 514. The Spanish painter Mariano Fortuny (1838–74) made a charcoal drawing, *Study for a Crucifixion*, at Gigi's Academy in 1860. For this and other works in oil, pen, and watercolor made by Fortuny at Gigi's, see Begoña Torres González, *Fortuny: Un mundo en miniatura* (Madrid: Editorial LIBSA, 2008), 172–73. A similar sketch by Adrien de Witte is reproduced in Dupont, *Modèles italiens*, 2:xv.

50. Ibid., 514–15.

51. Ibid., 515–16.

52. Leland, *Americans*, 106.

53. H. M. B., from *Once a Week* as quoted in Augustus J. C. Hare, *Walks in Rome* 5th ed. (London: Daldy, Isbister and Co., 1876), 55.

54. Ibid.

55. "Journey," *Bentley's*, 512.

56. David Maitland Armstrong, *Day before Yesterday: Reminiscences of a Varied Life*, ed. Margaret Armstrong (New York: Charles Scribner's Sons, 1920), 196. The word *mollica* was misspelled in Armstrong's book as "moulika."

57. Ibid., 196–97.

58. James E. Freeman, *Gatherings from an Artist's Portfolio* (New York: D. Appleton and Company, 1877), 204–05.

59. William Gardiner, *Sights in Italy* (London: Longman, Brown, Green, and Longmans, 1847), 235.

60. Grace Greenwood, *Haps and Mishaps of a Tour in Europe* (Boston: Ticknor, Reed, and Fields, 1854), 249–50.

61. Gardiner, *Sights*, 111–12.

62. Numerous fiction and non-fiction literary accounts exist on Beppo. The American artist Felix O. C. Darley drew a caricature of Beppo for his travel memoirs, *Sketches Abroad with Pen and Pencil* (New York: Hurd and Houghton, 1868), 160.

63. Hans Christian Andersen, *The Improvisatore: or, Life in Italy*, trans. Mary Howitt (London: Richard Bentley, 1847), 5.

64. Nathaniel Hawthorne, *The Marble Faun: or, The Romance of Monte Beni*, 2 vols. (Boston: Ticknor and Fields, 1860), 1:143.

65. Leonora Cranch Scott, *The Life and Letters of Christopher Pearse Cranch* (Boston: Houghton, Mifflin Co., 1917), 235.

66. Freeman, *Gatherings* 1877, 133.

67. Ibid., 128.

68. Ibid., 127.

69. Ibid., 133.

70. Ibid., 261–62.

71. Charles Richard Weld, *Last Winter in Rome* (London: Longman, Green, Longman, Roberts, and Green, 1865), 391.

72. Freeman, *Gatherings* 1877, 208–09.

*Above right*

Fig. 92. SCENERY FOUND. not dated

John Gadsby Chapman (1808–1889)
Oil on wooden artist's palette
11 ⅛ x 8 ½ in. (28.2 x 21.6 cm)
Private collection

# American Open-Air Landscape Painting in Rome, 1825–1885

JOHN F. McGUIGAN JR.

In the nearly sixty years since *Travelers in Arcadia: American Artists in Italy 1830–1875*—Edgar P. Richardson and Otto Wittmann Jr.'s pioneering 1951 exhibition—appeared, almost a dozen similar endeavors have been devoted to the rich topic of New World artists who studied on the Italian peninsula in the nineteenth century. Recognition of the seminal importance of the Italian sojourn culminated with Theodore E. Stebbins Jr.'s monumental 1992 undertaking, *The Lure of Italy: American Artists and the Italian Experience, 1760–1914*, for the Museum of Fine Arts, Boston. Despite the undeniable significance of these exhibitions, they have focused mainly on paintings made in the studio and have largely marginalized oil sketches executed in the open air on paper, canvas, artist board, or wood panel. These small paintings trained artists to quickly and accurately record the natural world and the transitory effects of atmosphere and light on color and form. Painters later referred to their oil sketches for inspiration and compositional elements when producing larger, more highly finished canvases in their studios back in Rome or the United States. Coincident with the recent scholarly reappraisal of the European practice of open-air painting, now is an opportune moment to assess the contribution of nineteenth-century Americans in Rome and properly resituate them within their international milieu.[1]

Rome is generally recognized as the birthplace of open-air painting in the mid-seventeenth century, at the hands of Claude Lorrain (1604/5–82), Salvator Rosa (1615–73), and others. However, because so few of these prototypical sketches survive, it is difficult to determine to what extent the Roman tradition flourished until it gained prominence in the mid- to late-eighteenth century, with most experts settling on the early 1780s for its widespread dissemination. The tradition codified into a discipline as masters indoctrinated their students in the idiom, epitomized by the paradigm of four generations of French painters: Claude-Joseph Vernet (1714–89), Pierre-Henri de Valenciennes (1750–1819), Achille-Etna Michallon (1796–1822), and Jean-Baptiste-Camille Corot (1796–1875).

The open-air oil sketch may be seen to have reached its apogee in Corot's oeuvre from his first Italian trip from 1825 to 1828, especially the examples he created in the environs of Rome. Although a number of American painters resided in the city contemporaneously with Corot and painted the same locations, they have been all but excluded from the chronicles of the golden age of open-air painting in Rome. The art historian Peter Galassi perpetuated this historical inaccuracy in his influential 1981 catalogue *Before Photography*, where he wrote, "Conspicuously absent are the Americans, who lacked the conditioning environment of tradition. The earliest American oil sketches, comparable to those common in Europe from 1780, were made in the late 1840s, when European practice had already begun to change."[2] Eleanor Jones Harvey did much to refute this in her 1998 exhibition catalogue *The Painted Sketch: American Impressions from Nature 1830–1880*, in which she established that the form was in limited usage in the United States in the first half of the 1820s. This early date is significant because it signals a cognizance of the practice in the American artistic community prior to the period under discussion here. Nevertheless, the late Philip Conisbee only fleetingly acknowledged Harvey's pioneering contribution in his 2004 essay for *Plein-Air Painting in Europe 1780–1850* by slightly qualifying Galassi's argument to allow that "as the 19th century progressed, the phenomenon spread beyond Europe, so that American painters were soon to be included among the open-air oil sketchers."[3]

*Left*
Fig. 93. FLORENCE
BY MOONLIGHT, 1825
(not in exhibition)
Robert Walter Weir (1803–1889)
Oil on panel
5 x 8 ¼ in. (12.7 x 21 cm)
Private collection

Although I would like to present a comprehensive survey of American open-air painting in Rome, I am constrained by the peregrinations of the art market through which these little gems have quietly changed hands among myriad owners over the last one hundred and fifty years. Filtered through that process, the landscapes in this exhibition emerged from a variety of sources: some sold out of the studio; some consigned en masse to public auction, as Jasper Francis Cropsey (1823–1900) and George Loring Brown (1814–89) did in 1856 and 1879 respectively; and some dispersed later by descendants, as in the case of Thomas Cole (1800–48), John Gadsby Chapman (1808–89), William Holbrook Beard (1824–1900), Jervis McEntee (1828–91), and Albert Bierstadt (1830–1902),

*Above*

Fig. 94. TEMPLE OF VESTA, ROME, ca. 1826

Robert Walter Weir (1803–1889)
Graphite, pen and ink, and
ink wash on buff wove paper
7 ¼ x 10 in. (18.4 x 25.4 cm)
Private collection

among others. Thus, by necessity I can only discuss the open-air paintings that fortune has favored us with and those artists who left clues to their work habits.

Oil painting outdoors was a laborious and cumbersome proposition, particularly before Winsor & Newton began marketing the collapsible paint tube in 1842. Prior to that, artists had to grind their own pigments, mix them in oil, and carefully pour them into delicate animal bladders to transport them into the field. Add to this the other heavy accoutrements of the trade—umbrella to filter sunlight, campstool, easel, and box holding a palette, brushes, and canvas, panel, or paper. Despite the burdensome inconvenience, it did little to daunt the eager student of nature. By the time Robert Walter Weir (1803–89) arrived in Rome in December 1825 for two years of study, he was already well-versed in the rigors that oil painting presented. He credited his preparedness to his early experiences in New York City, where "you could buy neither colors nor canvas." Rather, he explained, "As in the time of the old masters, you had to buy the rough materials and grind them up yourself, and to stretch your own canvas. One single apothecary shop, in Chatham Street, kept art materials."[4]

Although he initially found Rome inhospitable, once Weir was settled and fluent in the language he conceded that it was the "most delightful place I have ever been."[5] Weir's documented Roman output indicates an equal study of nature as well as of the figure. On a typical day he might draw at the French Academy,

*Above*

Fig. 95. SELF-PORTRAIT
LOOKING FOR SCENERY, not dated

John Gadsby Chapman (1808–1889)
Etching
3 x 2 ½ in. (7.6 x 6.4 cm)
Private collection

*Below*

Fig. 96. SELF-PORTRAIT
PAINTING OUTDOORS, not dated

John Gadsby Chapman (1808–1889)
Etching
3 ½ x 2 ½ in. (8.9 x 6.4 cm)
Private collection

socialize at the Caffè Greco (as did Corot), paint in his studio or sketch in nature, and work from the living model at the English Academy at night. Paintings later exhibited at the National Academy of Design in New York City, such as *View in Rome, Moonlight in the Colosseum, View from a Convent Gate near Rome,* and *Sunset, a View near Rome* (all unlocated), reveal his fascination with the *genius loci* of Rome. While little of Weir's early work has surfaced, one oil sketch entitled *Florence by Moonlight* (fig. 93) is indicative of his skillful execution. Furthermore, his detailed drawing of *Temple of Vesta, Rome* (fig. 94) attests to his refined sensibilities as a draftsman in the field, employing different media—graphite as well as ink applied with both brush and pen—to achieve a luminous effect.

In 1828 John Gadsby Chapman began a two-and-a-half-year course of study in Rome, and his surviving oil sketches and the historical record, which lists many lost works described as "painted on the spot," indicate that, like Weir, he was already adept at open-air painting.[6] From his writings we can deduce that Chapman avoided painting landscapes in the studio, preferring to work outdoors throughout his beloved Rome, the city to which he would expatriate twenty-two years later. In his popular educational treatise, *The American Drawing-Book: A Manual for the Amateur* (first published 1847), Chapman stated that one advantage of the latter type of facture was the cultivation of a discriminating eye:

> The exercise of much judgment will be often called in requisition in painting in the open air, from the variations of light on objects, and other causes. In the studio, the light on an object may be retained with little variation throughout the day; while in the open air, and particularly in sunlight, it is constantly changing, so that in the course of a few hours the general effect may be entirely altered.[7]

As the working conditions changed over the course of the day, Chapman recommended that "more than one sketch or study should be carried on at the same time, or rather in the same excursion. Thus, in the morning we may progress with one study, and in the afternoon with another. To this end, sketch-boxes are so contrived as to carry several sketches at once, in an undried state, without injury."[8]

Another American resident in Rome in 1829 was Rembrandt Peale (1778–1860), a scion of the Pennsylvania family of painters. For the most part Peale remained in the city overseeing the education of his teenage son Michael Angelo (1814–33) and showing a version of his portrait of George Washington to great acclaim at the Porta del Popolo Exhibition in Rome. Nevertheless, Peale did manage to venture to nearby Tivoli in May 1830 to sketch its famous waterfalls:

> Having the convenience of a landscape painter's travelling apparatus, I descended with some difficulty the steep side of the mountain, holding on to clusters of rushes, till I found among the rocks and bushes, on the precipice below, a mule path, leading to a small cultivated spot, whence I could command a fine view of the Cascatelles. . . . Seated on my three legged stool, the paint box in my lap, I hastened to record in colours the scene of enchantment before me; whilst the little bare-headed village boy, with my umbrella, kept off the bright and burning rays of the sun, and, occasionally, the spray from the falls.[9] (fig. 96)

*Above*
Fig. 97. SHEPHERD BOY
RESCUING LAMB, not dated
John Gadsby Chapman (1808–1889)
Oil on wooden artist's palette
11 ⅛ x 8 ½ in. (28.2 x 21.6 cm)
Private collection

In his *Notes on Italy*, published the following year, Peale made a distinction between open-air oil painting at home and abroad that assumed his readers' familiarity with the practice: "In America such cultivated spots would have their inhabitants, in whose huts the artist might seek some occasional refreshment, or leave his materials till the next day, or during a shower." That was not the case in Tivoli, however, where the farm workers all lived up in the hill town, not near the fields they tended. "Artists, therefore, who study in these solitudes suffer many inconveniences," he lamented. Peale painted for four days in Tivoli, staying at a favorite haunt of artists, the Inn of the Sibyls, where, he wrote, "the walls of my bed-room were inscribed with columns of their signatures, and exclamations of delight at the charms of Tivoli."[10]

In February 1830 Samuel Finley Breese Morse (1791–1872), the president of the National Academy of Design, arrived in Rome. He frequently visited the French Academy and attended an exhibition there in April that consisted of "13

*Below*

Fig. 98. GOING TO REST
FOR THE NIGHT, 1830

John Gadsby Chapman (1808–1889)
Oil on wood panel
6 ⅜ x 8 ½ in. (16.2 x 21.6 cm)
Private collection

pictures and a frame containing 20 landscape sketches from nature" that piqued his interest. Morse singled out works by members of Corot's circle, Louis Dupré (1789–1837), the pensioners Charles-Philippe de Larivière (1798–1876) and François Bouchot (1800–42), and André Giroux (1801–79), whose "small sketches," he noted, were "all full of nature."[11] Thus displaying an early enthusiasm for the aesthetic merits of outdoor paintings, we should not be surprised that Morse noted in his diary his and Chapman's preparations for their own open-air work, namely, "equipping ourselves in our traveling costume and painting paraphernalia, viz. a box of colors &c slung over the shoulders like a knapsack by a strap, an umbrella, and field chair."[12]

Morse and Chapman embarked on an extended sketching excursion to the Castelli Romani on May 4, 1830, proceeding to Tivoli, Vicovaro, and Subiaco, where a large contingent of foreign artists was already installed. Indeed, oil sketchers were so ubiquitous in Italy that Chapman forewarned his American audience:

> In the Old World, out-of-door study is carried to a much greater extent than with us. The traveler is for ever reminded that the artist is abroad; and scarcely a picturesque spot he visits, but he will find either the well-equipped amateur, beneath his camp-umbrella, fortified at all points, and against all emergencies, with patent contrivances and conveniences, or the more business-like artist, with his well-worn sketch-box or portfolio. He may be, not infrequently, startled by meeting, on his way, some strangely-caparisoned and even uncouth-looking figure, on foot or mounted on that much-abused yet patient bearer of all burdens, outward or homeward bound on some expedition in search of the beautiful, and possibly he may be no less surprised to recognize therein one world-famed in art.[13] (fig. 95)

*Below*
Fig. 101. STUDY FOR
"THE DESOLATION." 1836
Thomas Cole (1801–1848)
Oil on wood panel
9 ¾ x 15 ⅝ in. (24.8 x 39.7 cm)
Private collection

Remaining at Subiaco several weeks the two men worked side by side, and we may compare Morse's *Sketch for "The Chapel of the Virgin at Subiaco"* (fig. 99)—the model for what he considered to be his most successful landscape to date, *The Chapel of the Virgin at Subiaco* (1830–31, Worcester Art Museum)—with Chapman's *Going to Rest for the Night* (fig. 98), which likely dates from this same trip. In his painting, Morse portrayed several figures against the dramatic backdrop of the rugged hill town in the effulgent light of early evening. A shepherd and contadina with their nearby flock stop at a wayside shrine to say their evening prayers, while a Benedictine monk and another contadina, balancing a *conca*, or copper water vessel, on her head, descend the hill. Chapman set his scene at dusk, with a shepherd returning his flock to their damp, cavernous domicile while a contadina has just filled her *conca* from a cistern. Both evince tremendous technical skill in painting outdoors, but Morse's may be more comfortably situated within the contemporary European interest in direct observation and the effects of light and atmosphere, whereas Chapman's is decidedly more theatrical in its treatment of the shallow, dimly lit space and is indebted thematically to the dramatic oeuvre of Salvator Rosa.

After only two weeks back in Rome, Chapman and Morse returned to the Castelli Romani on June 16, 1830. Their destination this time was the famous Genzano *Infiorata*, or flower festival, to be held the following day. For their base they chose the Locanda Martorelli, a humble inn in Ariccia that had been welcoming the bohemian set since it opened ten years earlier. The New York figure painter James Edward Freeman (1808–84), a frequent guest there during his nearly fifty-year residence in Italy, wrote that the inn "often had for its guests Vernet, Cornelius, Gibson, and other celebrated artists. I have seen traces of the genius of some of these eminent men in rough sketches upon the walls of the bedrooms where they slept."[14] Arriving at ten o'clock in the morning, Morse recorded that the "locanda of Signore Martorelli . . . was so crowded with artists (22 being at table and all English and American except 2), that there were not beds enough to accommodate all in the house."[15] The large number of painters in search of the picturesque migrated to Genzano the next day for the *Infiorata*,

where, Morse noted, "we found . . . not less than 150 artists of all nations from
Rome; the German artists making the most conspicuous figure having their
portfolios and camp chairs slung like a knapsack at their backs."[16]

After Chapman and Peale returned to the United States, and Morse moved
to Paris, Thomas Cole and Francis Alexander (1800–80) arrived in Rome in
February 1832 and took a studio in the "very house in which Claude lived."[17]
Prior to that, Cole had spent the previous two and a half years studying in London—where he entered the circles of two of England's most versatile and prolific
oil sketchers, J. M. W. Turner (1775–1851) and John Constable (1776–1837)—
Paris, and Florence. Cole's biographer, Louis Legrand Noble (1813–82),
recognized that "Roman nature then was to him as another Vatican or St. Peter's
infinitely expanded, into which he now went forth with palette and portfolio."[18]

From the journal of John Cranch (1807–91), his traveling companion to Volterra in the Tuscan countryside in August 1831, we learn that Cole was an experienced and proficient open-airist: "Mr. C[ole] produced something very beautiful. I, who am not at all experienced in painting in this way, made a poor daub."[19] On another occasion Cranch recounted, "I made a bad sketch in oil. C[ole] made an excellent one."[20] Cranch further reported that Cole continued to work on his field sketches back in his rooms. For his part, Cole committed to his journal, "I have labored hard since I have been at Volterra—sallying forth with my sketch book or paint box every morning at five and never returning until night."[21]

Although Cole reveled in many aspects of Rome's palimpsest of architecture—the modern cityscape, the Campagna's medieval farmhouses, the organic evolution of the hill towns—he confided to his parents that the "things that most affect me, in Rome, are the antiquities. None but those who can see the remains can form an idea of what ancient Rome was."[22] The Colosseum in particular, he declared, surpassed all others in sublimity:

*Below*
Fig. 105. THE FALLS
AT TIVOLI, 1846
John Frederick Kensett (1816–1872)
Oil on paper on canvas
9 ¾ x 14 ½ in. (24.7 x 36.8 cm)
Private collection

*Above*

Fig. 106. SUNSET AT OLEVANO, 1848

Jasper Francis Cropsey (1823–1900)

Oil on paper on canvas

5 ½ x 8 ¹/₁₆ in. (13.4 x 20.4 cm)

Private collection

*Opposite*

Fig. 107. VIEW IN L'ARICCIA, 1848

Jasper Francis Cropsey (1823–1900)

Oil on canvas

10 ¼ x 14 in. (26 x 35.5 cm)

Private collection

It is stupendous, yet beautiful in its destruction. From the broad arena within, it rises around you, arch above arch, broken and desolate, and mantled in many parts with the laurustinus, the acanthus, and numerous other plants and flowers, exquisite both for their color and fragrance. It looks more like a work of nature than of man; for the regularity of art is lost, in a great measure, in dilapidation, and the luxuriant herbage, clinging to its ruins as if to "mouth its distress," completes the illusion. Crag rises over crag, green and breezy summits mount into the sky. To walk beneath its crumbling walls, to climb its shattered steps, to wander through its long, arched passages, to tread in the footsteps of Rome's ancient kings, to muse upon its broken height, is to lapse into sad, though not unpleasing meditation.[23]

Cole successfully evoked the exquisite melancholy of the location in his *Interior of the Colosseum, Rome* (fig. 17), a picture that presents a conundrum as to whether it was painted *in situ*, in the manner of Morse and Chapman, or in the studio, based on drawings and memory. It possesses such a remarkable freshness and almost palpable sense of wonder—qualities that characterize many of Cole's open-air oil sketches—that I am inclined to think it was painted on the spot. Furthermore, it bears little stylistic resemblance to Cole's wholly imaginary *Study for "The Desolation"* (fig. 101), which he executed in his Catskill, New York, studio as a preparatory study for *The Desolation*, the emphatic culmination of his five-picture cycle, *The Course of Empire* (1836, New-York Historical Society). It is significant to note, nevertheless, that Cole's initial vision for *The Course of Empire* dates to his residence in Rome:

Returning, once, from a long walk with a few friends, he seated himself on the fragments of a column to enjoy the sunset. As its splendors faded into the twilight, all lapsed into a stillness suited to the solemn repose peculiar, at that time, to a scene of ruin. There came through the deepening shadows few sounds louder than the beating of their hearts. After some minutes of silent, mournful pleasure, seated a little apart by a lady, Cole, a thing rather unusual with him, was the first to speak. This he did in his own low, quiet voice, but with such earnestness as told the depth of his emotions, and the greatness of his thoughts. The subject was that of the future *Course of Empire*. In his own brief and simple way, he passed from point to point in the series, making, by many a clear and vivid outline, the liveliest impression upon the mind of his listener, until he closed with a picture that found its parallel in the melancholy desolation by which, at that moment, they were surrounded. Such was Cole, the poet artist, at Rome.[24]

Noble understood that for Cole in Rome, "a grander book had opened: he read its profounder lessons, and felt assured and free to enter upon his task."[25] The idea that ancient ruins could be morally didactic as the vestiges of the rise and fall of empire—of the rise and fall of man's hubris—does, ultimately, unite Cole's oil sketch of the Colosseum with his oil study and final canvas of *The Desolation*.

Later in life, Cole downplayed ever having painted outdoors and claimed to work almost exclusively from his imagination after careful study of nature. As early as 1835 he professed in a letter to one of his patrons, Robert Gilmor Jr. (1774–1848) of Baltimore, that his open-air sketches were "*generally* mere outlines" and that his methodology was essentially meditative:

*Below*
Fig. 108. LOOKING TOWARD TIVOLI FROM FRASCATI, 1855
George Loring Brown (1814–1889)
Oil on board
12 ⅝ x 19 ⅜ in. (31.1 x 47.6 cm)
Private collection

My desire & endeavor is always to get the objects of nature, sky, rocks,
trees, &c—as strongly impressed on my mind as possible & by looking
intently on an object for twenty minutes I can go to my room & paint
it with much more truth, than I could if I employed several hours on
the spot. By this means I become more intimately acquainted with
the characteristics of the spirit of Nature than I could otherwise do.[26]

It was a claim that found amazing traction among Cole's professional colleagues.
Chapman—an intimate of his—proclaimed that Cole "rarely, if ever" participated
in the "almost universal practice of out-door study of Nature" and grouped him
with others who, "by strength of memory, or other natural or acquired qualifi-
cations, have successfully secured by other means the advantages of such study."[27]
John Durand (1822–1908), art critic and founder of an influential journal, the
*Crayon*, legitimized the idea when he elevated his father, Asher B. Durand (1796–
1886), to the status of the first American to paint outdoors in his biography

of him. And Thomas Worthington Whittredge (1820–1910), perhaps attempting to establish his own generation's primacy as the originators of the oil sketch in America, perpetuated this revisionist history when he stated that "nobody, not even Cole, had, up to that time, ever attempted to paint out-of-doors."[28]

What are we to make of Cole's mythopoetry in light of the substantial evidence—namely, his considerable oeuvre of well-developed open-air oil sketches—that contradicts it?[29] I contend that the painter was intentionally attempting to cast himself in the image of Claude Lorrain, the old master most esteemed in nineteenth-century Anglo-American art circles. Reconsider Cole's assertion above after reading what Joachim von Sandrart (1606–88), Claude's colleague and biographer, said about his subject's approach to painting in the outdoors:

> He tried by every means to penetrate nature, lying in the fields before the break of day and until night in order to learn to represent very exactly the red morning-sky, sunrise and sunset and the evening hours. When he had well contemplated one or the other in the fields, he immediately prepared his colors accordingly, returned home, and applied them to the work he had in mind with much greater naturalness than anyone had ever done.[30]

*Below*

Fig. 111. MONTE GENNARO FROM HADRIAN'S VILLA, ca. 1856–57

Albert Bierstadt (1830–1902)
Oil on paper on board
7 x 19 ½ in. (17.8 x 49.5 cm)
Private collection

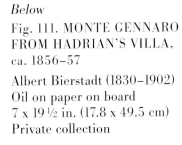

*Opposite*

Fig. 110. VILLA D'ESTE, TIVOLI, 1856

Thomas Worthington Whittredge (1820–1910)
Oil on canvas
15 ¾ x 12 in. (40 x 30.5 cm)
Private collection

Claude did eventually paint in the outdoors after a fateful encounter with Sandrart, who recalled how "he finally met me, brush in hand, at Tivoli, in the wild rocks of the famous cascade, where he found me painting from life, and saw that I painted many works from nature itself, making nothing from imagination; this pleased him so much that he applied himself eagerly to adopting the same method." Nevertheless, Sandrart stipulated that the "perfection" of Claude's landscapes resulted from "exceeding laboriousness, frequently repeated overpaints, examinations, and going over them again, so that he often works one or two weeks on a thing."[31] Again, compare this with how Cole couched his language in his concluding remarks to Gilmor:

> I think that a vivid picture of any object in the mind's eye is worth a hundred finished sketches made on the spot—which are never more than half true—for the glare of light destroys the true effect

90

of colour & the tones of Nature are too refined to be obtained without repeated painting & glazings. And by my method I learn better
what Nature *is* & painting *ought to be*—get the philosophy of Nature
& Art—whereas a finished sketch may be done without obtaining
either one or the other—and is in great measure a mere mechanical
operation.[32]

Ultimately, the more one studies Cole's time in Italy, one sees just how closely
his identification with Claude is connected to his perception of his own advancement as an artist. Thus, when he ascended to Tivoli and its fabled waterfalls
on April 12, 1832, in the footsteps of Claude, it was with the reverence of a
pilgrim. Evidence of Cole's devotional attitude can be found in his dramatic
exhibition-sized composition, *The Cascatelli, Tivoli, Looking towards Rome*
(fig. 29), which is strongly reminiscent of Claude's *View of the Campagna from
Tivoli* (1645, H. M. the Queen).[33]

*Above*
Fig. 114. STUDY FOR
"AMPHITHEATER
AT TUSCULUM AND
ALBANO MOUNTAINS,
ROME." ca. 1856–59
Thomas Worthington Whittredge
(1820–1910)
Oil on paper on board
10 ½ x 16 ⅜ in. (26.7 x 41.6 cm)
Private collection

*Above*

Fig. 115. COUNTRY FAIR AT GROTTA FERRATA, 1857

William Holbrook Beard (1824–1900). Oil on paper on board.
9 x 12 in. (22.9 x 30.5 cm). Private collection

*Opposite above and below*

Fig. 117. BOY WITH A KNIFE, GENAZZANO, 1857

Peter Frederick Rothermel (1817–1895). Oil on pale gray wove paper
11 x 8 ¼ in. (27.9 x 20.9 cm). Private collection

Fig. 116. ROOFTOPS AT GENAZZANO, 1857

Peter Frederick Rothermel (1817–1895). Oil on blue wove paper
8 ¼ x 11 in. (21 x 27.9 cm). Private collection

*The Tomb of Caius Cestius, Rome* (fig. 102), by Alfred Jacob Miller (1810–74), shares many of the romantic qualities of Cole's works, especially his *Study for "The Desolation."* Miller's view of the ancient pyramidal mausoleum that mournfully presides over Testaccio, Rome's Protestant Cemetery, with the city wall and Porta San Paolo behind it, bathed in the mellow glow of the setting sun, is, on closer inspection, punctuated with figures of mourners filing past the grave of the English poet John Keats (1795–1821) on their way to a funeral. It is worthwhile to compare Miller's picture with Cole's of the same subject, *Study for "The Protestant Burying Ground, Rome"* (1832, Private collection).[34] Whereas Miller entered the cemetery's enclosure, unafraid of what it represents, Cole, on the other hand, preferred to keep it at a distance, situating a lone figure at a remote, elevated perspective, safely removed from the terrestrial reminder of man's mortality.

From Weir, Chapman, and Peale in the 1820s, through Morse, Cole, and Miller in the early 1830s, I have established that the Americans were learned regular participants within the international community of open-airists based in Rome in the early decades of the nineteenth century. Thus, in my ensuing discussion about the 1840s and beyond—decades in which landscapists constituted the

majority of the colony of American painters resident there—I safely assume that subsequent generations were informed about the widespread practice of oil painting under the canopy of Rome's felicitous sky and prepared to take part. Therefore, as I proceed chronologically, the focus shifts to how some of America's foremost painters perceived the Italian landscape and their different approaches to rendering it.

In October 1845 John F. Kensett (1816–72), a gifted engraver and aspiring painter from Connecticut, came to Rome after five years of study in England and France. As one nineteenth-century critic observed, Kensett had yet to distinguish himself as a landscapist: "He had studied the French styles, and copied them. He had studied the German styles, and copied them. He had given up his own originality altogether; and his work was a complete mannerism." In Rome, however, this same author reported, Kensett synthesized the merits of the various European schools into a wholly unique style. "This individuality," he concluded, "is the charm of all of his later work."[35] Why did Kensett's artistic epiphany occur in Rome, where the influences were as manifold, if not more so, as in London or Paris? I propose that Rome's benevolent climate and historically evocative scenery inspired him to formulate his own vision in solitude with nature.

In the instance of Kensett's *Gate to Cicero's Villa, Monte Albano* (fig. 103), painted in the summer of 1846 alongside Thomas Hicks (who added the two monks after the former man's untimely death in 1872), it was the classical association of the locale that attracted his brush. The simple arched gate in

the left foreground opens onto what was believed to be the ruins of the famed orator's country estate. One of the first open-air sketches that Kensett produced that summer, it attests to a general competency in painting in the field but also a rather conventional orientation to composition. By early October Kensett displayed greater freedom in *Town of Civitella, Italy* (fig. 104). His asymmetrical placement of the town perched atop a mountainous outcrop and his confident transition between thin and impasted brushwork indicate that the artist had gained in authority over the months. In a letter from the spot Kensett described Civitella's magnificent natural setting:

> Were you to stand at the entrance gate of the village with me and look around, you would see far off in the southwest the Alban range of mountains sweeping down into the broad Campagna and far as the eye could reach the dark blue Mediterranean. In the northwest the mountains of the Sabines fade in the distance, and in the east loom up the Apennines like sturdy giants watching their brood.[36]

*Right*
Fig. 122. ROCCA DI SECCA, 1858
Albert Bierstadt (1830–1902)
Oil on board
12 ½ x 18 ¾ in. (31.7 x 47.6 cm)
Private collection

98

*Opposite above*

Fig. 123. TORRE D'ASTURA,
not dated

John Gadsby Chapman (1808–1889)
Oil on board
7 x 14 in. (17.8 x 35.5 cm)
Private collection

*Opposite below*

Fig. 124. EXCAVATIONS
ON THE CAMPAGNA, 1854

John Gadsby Chapman (1808–1889)
Oil on canvas
33 ⅝ x 55 ⅝ in. (85.4 x 141.3 cm)
Private collection

*Above right*

Fig. 125. JOHN G. CHAPMAN
PAINTING A BUTTERBUR
FROM NATURE, ca. 1858

Conrad Wise Chapman (1842–1910)
Graphite on cream wove paper
5 x 8 ½ in. (12.7 x 21.6 cm)
Private collection

*Below right*

Fig. 126. BUTTERBUR PLANT,
CASTEL GANDOLFO, 1858

Conrad Wise Chapman (1842–1910)
Oil on paper on board
9 ¾ x 13 ½ in. (24.8 x 34.3 cm)
Private collection

Of his working habits, Kensett confided that "during my stay in the mountains I have been an early riser—4 o. c. in the morning, breakfasting and at my work ranging from 5 to ½ past 5. I have by this plan collected together many valuable sketches and studies in oil, some very large."[37]

Later that month Kensett and Hicks stopped in Tivoli, en route back to Rome. Kensett demonstrated the fruits of his summer labors in *The Falls at Tivoli* (fig. 105), in which multiple building facades and bridges run parallel to the picture plane and yet still convincingly suggest a recession in space. The seamless interplay of mass and void, light and shadow, organic and architectonic manifests a new level of comfort with the medium and the spontaneity of field work. Kensett's slow maturation as a landscape painter of singular originality ripened in Rome's fertile artistic environment, and, confident in his abilities, he returned to America to take his place among the first rank of his profession. His Italian oil studies continued to inform his career, as the

esteemed art critic George William Curtis (1824–92) nostalgically reflected, "There was no wall in New York so beautiful as that of his old studio . . . upon which they were hung in a solid mass."[38]

When Jasper F. Cropsey arrived in Rome from New York in October 1847, he engaged the same studio that Thomas Cole had occupied five years earlier on the Via del Babuino. One new acquaintance, the obscure American painter Thomas B. Ashton (dates unknown), described him as an "imitator of Cole but at a great distance."[39] Two of Cropsey's open-air paintings from 1848, *Sunset at Olevano* and *View in L'Ariccia* (figs. 106–107), reveal his indebtedness to Cole in their bravura technique, warm coloration, and crepuscular moodiness. Cropsey cultivated a romantic cast of mind not just in his art but in his writing, as when he related his impressions of the Claudian aqueducts to none other than Cole himself:

> Old arches, the bones of water bearers long ago, in long lines were shadowing over that lonely walk, so old and so lovely, with the sleepy shepherd and his scattered flock keeping them company— that I thought within myself, I love it, love it all, the campagna and the city, for their age. They seemed as a man trembling upon his staff, his thin locks silvered by time, and face deep wrinkled by care yet strong in the hope that lives forever.[40]

Margaret Fuller (1810–50), the noted writer and foreign correspondent for the *New-York Daily Tribune*, admired Cropsey's "true artist spirit." Her observation that "his pictures are full of little gentle signs of intimacy" reminds viewers to look closely for the shepherd and his flock in the left foreground of the first work and the lone figure of a cowled monk sequestered in the shady copse in the second.[41]

In 1845 the poet, scholar, and newspaper editor William Cullen Bryant (1794–1878) described George L. Brown as a "landscape painter of high merit," who "possesses great knowledge of detail, which he knows how to keep in its place, subduing it, and rendering it subservient to the general effect."[42] Although Brown produced many inspired, highly finished canvases, such as his enormous *Effect near Noon–along the Appian Way* (fig. 39), his reputation later suffered from his prodigious output of contrived and, frankly, derivative studio productions, many of which were executed by Italian assistants. However, the open-air

*Above*
Fig. 127. THE APPIAN WAY, 1869
John Linton Chapman (1839–1905)
Oil on canvas
29 7/16 x 71 9/16 in (74.7 x 181.7 cm)
Brooklyn Museum, Gift of The Roebling Society, Carll H. de Silver Fund, Caroline H. Polhemus Fund, A. Augustus Healy Fund, Frederick Loeser Fund, 79.87

oil sketches that he made during the nineteen years he passed on the Italian peninsula, beginning in 1840, comprise some of the finest work of his long career and, I believe, constitute his most original contribution to the history of American art. For example, *Looking toward Tivoli from Frascati* and *Study of Ilex Trees, Rocca di Papa* (figs. 108–109), both dating from the summer he spent in the latter town in 1855, evince an immediacy that had virtually ceased to exist in his studio paintings by this time. Moreover, Brown's expert handling of paint glazes has seldom found parallel and truly proves him a master of the medium.

By the mid-1850s the apartment and adjoining studio of the figure and fancy picture painter James E. Freeman, centrally located at Via Capo le Case 68, served as one the more prominent meeting places for the American artistic colony—aside from the perennially popular Caffè Greco. One noteworthy feature of Freeman's apartments was the choice collection of preparatory oil studies that he had assembled from his European and American contemporaries in Italy. An avid open-airist who regularly sketched the picturesque peasants and scenic natural beauty of his adopted homeland, Freeman alluded to the camaraderie with one's peers that frequently accompanied the practice in his homage to artist life in Italy, *Costume Picture* (fig. 91). In a gesture of his esteem, he painted the likenesses of the American landscapists William Stanley Haseltine (1835–1900) and Worthington Whittredge, the latter man with a stretched canvas peeking out of his knapsack, on the far left side of the composition. They chance upon another painter (essentially a substitution for

*Below*
Fig. 128. CLAUDIAN AQUEDUCT, ca. 1870
John Linton Chapman (1839–1905)
Oil on canvas
14 x 28 in. (35.5 x 71.1 cm)
Private collection

*Below*

Fig. 129. SKETCH OF GOATS,
ROME, 1857

Joseph C. Ropes (1812–1885)
Graphite on cream wove paper
8 x 10 ¼ in. (20.32 x 26 cm)
Private collection

*Below*

Fig. 130. LANDSCAPE
AT FRATTOCCHIE, 1861

Conrad Wise Chapman (1842–1910)
Oil on paper on canvas
4 ⅝ x 15 1/16 in. (11.7 x 38.3 cm)
Private collection

Freeman himself) surrounded by the tools of his trade—paint box (with a completed landscape sketch pinned to the inside lid), collapsible easel, and camp-stool—as he sketches a little girl. The setting is Ariccia, not far from the Locanda Martorelli, where Freeman was a regular summer resident.

Haseltine and Whittredge were the first of a contingent of landscape painters to descend on Rome from Düsseldorf, Germany, in the winter of 1856; Albert Bierstadt, William H. Beard, and Sanford Robinson Gifford (1823–80) would arrive shortly thereafter. Under the auspices of Professor Johann Wilhelm Schirmer (1807–63), Düsseldorf with its academy became a leading center for indoctrinating students in open-air oil painting. Haseltine's *The Roman Campagna, View toward Rome* (fig. 24) is a masterful example, focusing on amorphous ruins in the immediate foreground, yet suggesting the panoramic vastness of the sun-drenched countryside with the city skyline on the far horizon. Whittredge, the eldest of this group, frequently acted as a mentor to his fellow students, and when he ventured forth on open-air expeditions, they often followed. Whittredge described one occasion with particular gusto for its bohemian aspects:

> I lived a little while at Nemi on the Lake of [Nemi] and slept every night in the famous bed of the very little but very old inn, the only inn in the place and the only bed in the inn. It was of enormous size and kept as neat and clean as any bed in the best hotels. In fact, it was a kind of ancient advertisement for the insignificant town of Nemi, which the landlord thoroughly understood. Myself, Gifford, William Beard, Haseltine and Thomas Buchanan Read, author of "Sheridan's Ride," all slept in it one night, while making a pedestrian excursion around the lake, and there was room for one more.[43]

Of his four years' labor in Rome Whittredge recalled, "I worked away making studies on the Campagna and in the Alban and Sabine mountains, converting my studies into pictures."[44] His *Study for "Amphitheater at Tusculum and Albano Mountains"* (fig. 114) focuses exclusively on the undulations and natural depressions of the topography, while ignoring the ancient ruins, rudimentary

*capanna* (or peasant hut), staffage figures, and vegetation that litter the foreground of the finished painting (1859, Smithsonian American Art Museum).[45]

Whittredge's *Villa d'Este, Tivoli* (fig. 110) is an interesting example of a *contre-jour*, or backlit, effect, with the diffuse rays of the late-afternoon sun emanating from behind the imposing facade of the famed grand tour destination and glimpsing through the cypresses that flank the *allée*. Bierstadt's *Monte Gennaro from Hadrian's Villa* (fig. 111) likely dates from this same trip to Tivoli. He provided a sense of scale against which the distant monolith may be gauged by adding the merest suggestion of a village and a plume of smoke in the middle distance, and, most notably, a solitary cypress that pierces the bottom of the composition and indicates the foreground. These details, abbreviated and subtle as they may be to the untrained eye, were effective visual memoranda of a specific time and place and reveal Bierstadt to be a shrewd observer-recorder.

"The winter in Rome has been about as unpleasant as it could be. For sixty days we have scarcely had a fine one," Gifford dolefully apprised his father on February 5, 1857. He continued, however, that "yesterday this long spell of gloomy weather was broken by a bright, genial, sunny day."[46] The improved climate prompted the peripatetic Gifford to resume working from nature, and he set out on foot with Beard for the Campagna. *The Roman Campagna* (fig. 21) is a later studio version of an oil sketch made on one such outing to the Claudian aqueducts, which he would have first drawn in his sketchbook and then, happy with the idea, painted *in situ* (the first recorded occasion was November 3, 1856).[47] This was the artist's usual methodology, committing himself only briefly to a thumbnail drawing of a scene and returning later to paint it. The oil sketch, we are told by a contemporary critic, was the crucial creative stage for Gifford: "He experiments with it; puts in or leaves out, according as he finds that he can increase or perfect his idea. When satisfactorily finished, it is a model in miniature of what he proposes to do."[48]

On March 25, 1857, Gifford and Beard convened at 5:30 in the morning for the thirteen-mile journey from Rome to Grotta Ferrata to attend a celebrated country fair. Bierstadt and Virgil Williams (1830–86) joined them at Frascati for the last three miles. "The roads approaching Grotta Ferrata were thronged with peasants going to the fair," Gifford began his account of that day:

> Beggars without number lined the waysides. Arrived on the ground, the view presented was very interesting—a great variety of pictur-esque men and women (all in costumes peculiar to the different parts of the country in the vicinity they came from) with cattle, carts, horses, donkeys, &c. covered the rolling ground that extended up to the castellated towers and walls of the monastery of St. Basilio. Monte Cave, now half covered with a mist that threatened to spoil the day, made the background to the picture.[49]

Gifford's words found their visual equivalent in a small oil sketch, *Country Fair at Grotta Ferrata* (fig. 115), painted by Beard, whose close transcription of the foreground gathering of peasants, animals, and covered wagons in viscous strokes of paint yields to more generalized middle and backgrounds deftly conveyed by a broader, thinner handling. Based on the strength of this one painting alone we can appreciate the sentiment of the *Crayon's* foreign corre-spondent, who reported that summer that Beard had "shown great readiness in seizing the character of the landscape and peasantry."[50]

On April 22, 1857, Gifford departed Rome again with Julius O. de Montalant (1824–78), Jeremy Wilson (1824–99), and Peter Frederick Rothermel (1817–95) for the annual German artists' festival at the nearby caves at Cervara. The annual event was, the landscape painter and U.S. consul David Maitland Armstrong (1836–1918) noted, the "last spree of the season," effectively herald-ing the migration of painters from Rome to the surrounding hill towns for the malarial summer months.[51] Afterwards, Gifford planned a summer walking

*Below*
Fig. 132. RUINED CAPITALS
IN THE WOODS, ca. 1857–60
Elihu Vedder (1836–1923)
Oil on wood panel
5 5/16 x 12 11/16 in. (13.5 x 32.2 cm)
Private collection

tour with Bierstadt to Naples and Capri. He looked forward to encountering the people and rugged terrain of the Abruzzi region en route: "All the artists who have been there say it is the most Italian part of Italy. Strangers rarely ever go there." The two men left on May 13, 1857, intending to make "digressions among the mountains as the scenery &c. invites. We will shoulder our knapsacks and expect to rough it through in about a fortnight."[52] On his return to New Bedford, Massachusetts, Bierstadt immortalized their journey in *Rocca di Secca* (fig. 122), a view of a hill town on the border of the Papal States and the Kingdom of Naples. It is a finished oil study in which Bierstadt took the various drawings he made *in situ* and pieced them together—figures, trees, bridge, hamlet, and mountain—much like a jigsaw puzzle.

Rothermel passed that summer and fall in Genazzano, where he rendered landscape sketches "of the characteristics of Italian scenery for my own use hereafter," as well as "some sixty sketches of habits and customs of these very primitive people—those are of course hasty but quite sufficient for my use in case I wish hereafter to make pictures of the life in Italy."[53] His *Rooftops at Genazzano* (fig. 116) lyrically portrays the quotidian chores of drying laundry and threshing wheat against a tapestry of weathered stucco, terra cotta tiles, verdant hills, and distant azure mountains. Rothermel's extended commitment to recording the physiognomies, native dress, manners, and dwellings particular to the inhabitants of one small village partially stemmed from his training as a history painter, in which he strove for accuracy and authenticity in all the details of his compositions. That said, Rothermel's two-year Italian sojourn proved a watershed, as the *Crayon* astutely perceived: "He has made remarkable progress since his arrival in Europe. His works show a more earnest seeking after nature than formerly."[54]

When John Gadsby Chapman returned to the Eternal City in 1850, he brought his wife, daughter, and two protégés, his sons John Linton (1839–1905), or Jack, and Conrad Wise (1842–1910), with him. An 1856 visitor to the Chapman family's conjoined residence and studio at Via del Babuino 135 was delighted with the brilliant display on the walls. "Chapman is better known as a designer [draftsman] than a colorist, though his room contains sketches and pictures both of landscape and figure, which are clear and delicate in tint, and skillful in touch."[55] Many of John Gadsby's oil sketches remain unlocated, but one exceptional example that survives, *Torre d'Astura* (fig. 123), is a surprisingly compelling image despite its limited palette, modest dimensions, and humble subject matter. On a more monumental scale, his *Excavations on the Campagna* (fig. 124) leaves little doubt as to why he enjoyed a privileged reputation as one of America's most accomplished painters. It depicts a contemporary scene of more than a

*Below*
Fig. 134. PANORAMIC VIEW OF THE ROMAN CAMPAGNA, with Color Notations, 1861
Thomas Hiram Hotchkiss (1833–1869)
Pencil and black ink on off-white wove paper, in bound sketchbook
Sketchbook dimensions:
8 ¼ x 5 ⅝ x ½ in. (21 x 14.3 x 1.3 cm)
Private collection

*Left*

Fig. 135. NYMPHAEUM,
VILLA GORDIANI, 1861

Thomas Hiram Hotchkiss (1833–1869)
Watercolor on off-white wove paper,
in bound sketchbook
Sketchbook dimensions:
7 ½ x 5 ¾ x ¾ in. (19 x 14.6 x 2 cm)
Private collection

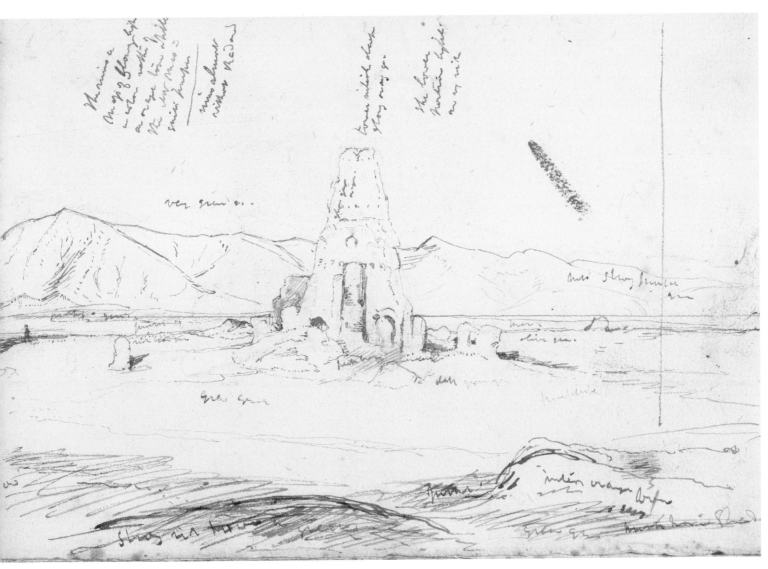

*Left*

Fig. 136. VIEW FROM
VIA SISTINA 72,
ROME, ca. 1874

Elihu Vedder (1836–1923)
Oil on canvas
12 5/8 x 7 5/8 in.
(32 x 19.4 cm)
Private collection

*Opposite above*

Fig. 137. VIEW OF
ST. PETER'S FROM
VIA DI RIPETTA IN
SKETCHBOOK NO. 5
(BIARRITZ TO ROME),
1880–81

Truman Seymour (1824–1891)
Graphite on buff wove paper
Sketchbook: 7 x 9 3/4 in.
(17.7 x 24.7 cm)
Private collection

dozen men working on a papally sanctioned archaeological dig at the ancient Villa Gordiani, with its famous *nymphaeum* and so-called Tor de' Schiavi in the middle distance. The verisimilitude that John Gadsby achieved in this and other *vedute*, large panoramic views, of Campagna life is reliant on the striking amount of detail he appropriated from drawings and oil sketches of mountain ridges, ruins, amphorae, oxen, and laborers that he amassed for just that purpose.

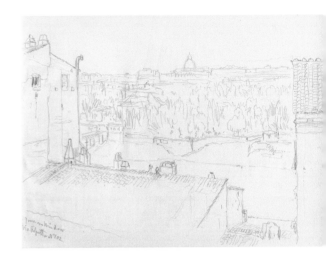

John Gadsby's sparse exhibition record belies the popularity of his Italian paintings with Americans. "Few of his works are visible in our exhibitions," a writer for the *Crayon* acknowledged, "but they are widely distributed through the country."[56] A painter, draftsman, engraver, and author, John Gadsby could not keep up with all his commissions and interests—try as he might. "Chapman is indefatigable," the art critic Henry Theodore Tuckerman (1813–71) marveled. "Early and late he is at work, and seems to overcome fatigue rather by changing his occupation than abstaining from labor."[57] So the artist who wrote that "any one who can learn to write can learn to draw" in *The American Drawing-Book* began instructing his sons Jack and Conrad, both of whom exhibited natural ability, in his profession.[58] Already by 1858 William Cullen Bryant reported from Rome that "Chapman's sons are both artists, and both show inclination and talent for painting. They begin to render very useful assistance to their father, and I always find them with the brush in their hands."[59]

One of the more visually exciting pairings in the present exhibition is Conrad Chapman's graphite sketch of *John G. Chapman Painting a Butterbur from Nature* (fig. 125) and his oil sketch of the same subject, *Butterbur Plant, Castel Gandolfo* (fig. 126), dated September 3, 1858. The painting is Conrad's earliest known open-air oil sketch, and it is not unreasonable to speculate that the drawing commemorates the occasion when his mentor initiated him into the pleasures and challenges of painting in nature. The drawing shows John Gadsby seated on a tripod stool, balancing his right arm on a maulstick as he daubs his paintbrush at a sheet of paper pinned to a sturdy board propped against the back of a chair. Conrad's lushly rendered close-up painting of the butterbur's enormous velvety leaves (he noted along the left margin that they measured fourteen inches) dwarfing nearby grasses, crocuses, and anemones is truly remarkable considering that

*Above*
Fig. 138. BRIDGE AT NARNI, 1867
Elihu Vedder (1836–1923)
Oil on canvas
6 ¼ x 16 in. (15.9 x 40.6 cm)
Private collection

*Below*

Fig. 139. BY THE TIBER NEAR
ROME, WINTER, ca. 1869–70

William Graham (1832–1911)
Oil on canvas on wood panel
11³⁄₁₆ x 6³⁄₈ in. (28.4 x 16.2 cm)
Private collection

*Right*

Fig. 140. WINTER
LANDSCAPE, 1870

Elihu Vedder (1836–1923)
Oil on paper on card
8³⁄₈ x 3¾ in. (21.3 x 9.5 cm)
Private collection

he was only sixteen years old at the time. It is easy to envision them side by side, the teacher painting next to his student, advising him, and perhaps adding to and correcting his work.

By 1861 Jack and Conrad were established members of the Roman art world with patron bases eager for their paintings of the rustic life in Italy (figs. 127, 128, and 131). The study of nature remained a high priority for both of them, getting them out into the field and informing their creative processes. Conrad's small *Landscape at Frattocchie* (fig. 130) reveals the continued influence of John Gadsby's *vedute* in the broad expanse of arable land, terminus of mountains, and sweeping view of white-clouded sky captured in thick, wet paint.

*Right*

Fig. 141. VIEW OF THE CAMPAGNA FROM THE BATHS OF CARACALLA, ca. 1872

Samuel Colman (1832–1920)
Oil on canvas
8 ³/₁₆ x 15 ⅛ in. (20.7 x 38.4 cm)
Private collection

*Below*

Fig. 142. BATHS OF CARACALLA, SANTA BALBINA, AND THE TOMB OF CAIUS CESTIUS FROM THE PALATINE HILL, 1877

Elihu Vedder (1836–1923)
Oil on canvas
5 ¾ x 20 ¼ in. (14.6 x 51.4 cm)
Private collection

It was a successful formula that Conrad adopted in many of his paintings of the American South and Mexico after he ran away in 1862 to fight for the Confederacy in the Civil War.

The second half of the 1860s witnessed a resurgence of Americans into the Eternal City. "An unusual number of American artists are spending this winter in Rome," *Putnam's Magazine* reported in 1869:

*Left*
Fig. 143. THE CLAUDIAN
AQUEDUCT AT TWILIGHT, 1869
Henry Augustus Loop (1831–1895)
Oil on canvas
7⅝ x 11⅝ in. (19.3 x 29.5 cm)
Private collection

In addition to those who permanently reside there—the sculptors Story, Rogers, Miss Stebbins, Harriet Hosmer, Miss Foley, and Mozier; the painters Terry, Tilton, Buchanan Read, Vedder, Coleman, Wild, and Hotchkiss—there will be a large accession to the number of temporary residents. Church and Bierstadt; Gifford and McEntee; Yewell, Loop, and other painters, and Launt Thompson, sculptor, have taken studios for the winter. Longfellow and Cyrus Field, with their families, will also form part of the American colony there.[60]

Now a Union veteran of the Civil War, Gifford spent most of his time nostalgically "going about in Rome and on the Campagna to review old familiar places and scenes."[61] Since he knew the country and its language, he assisted his friend

*Below*
Fig. 144. NYMPHAEUM AND
TOR DE' SCHIAVI,
VILLA GORDIANI, ca. 1872
Samuel Colman (1832–1920)
Oil on paper on board
7¼ x 4 in. (18.4 x 10.2 cm)
Private collection

*Above*
Fig. 145. OLD GATE AT NEMI, 1856
Henry Augustus Loop (1831–1895)
Oil on canvas
7 ½ x 11 ⅞ in. (19 x 30.1 cm)
Private collection

Jervis McEntee in getting settled. "As Mac does not yet speak a word of Italian, I act as his interpreter and dragoman generally. He is studying hard, and I think in a few weeks he will be able to look out for himself."[62] On October 13, Gifford journeyed to Tivoli with McEntee, who painted *Temple of Vesta, Tivoli* (fig. 133) there the following day. The artist employed a wet-on-wet technique, using flourishes of paint to suggest elegantly proportioned Corinthian columns, rusticated stonework, and hodgepodge of rooflines delineated against sky and verdant hills.

The economy with which McEntee quickly painted the view presented before him as a record for future reference lies in stark contrast to the pictorial concerns that motivated Elihu Vedder's (1836–1923) outdoor painting career, beginning with his first trip to Italy from 1857 to 1860, when he encountered members of the Macchiaioli, a loose affiliation of Italian (mostly Tuscan) landscape painters and dedicated open-airists. The flashes of distant blue sky and sliver of sunlit earth that alleviate the darkened seclusion of the grove in Vedder's *Ruined Capitals in the Woods* (fig. 132) are characteristic of the group's

employment of dashes of color (*macchia* is Italian for spot) to enliven a painting's surface. The almost pulsating chiaroscuro, or juxtaposition of light and shadow, reflects the Macchiaioli interest in maintaining the vigor and freshness of the initial artistic conception, or as Vedder phrased it: "What I felt strongly I could strongly express in the sketch, but the finished picture killed the feeling—and then in addition all became sicklied o'er by the pale cast of thought."[63] For Vedder and the Macchiaioli, the painted sketch was an end in itself.

*Above*

Fig. 146. ROMAN CAMPAGNA (PONTE NOMENTANO), ca. 1871

George Inness (1825–1894)
Oil on paper on board
8 ¾ x 13 ³⁄₁₆ in. (22.2 x 33.5 cm)
Private collection

*Left*

Fig. 147. VIEW OF AQUEDUCTS AT TWILIGHT, ca. 1884

John Severinus Conway (1852–1925)
Oil and graphite on wood panel
4 x 6 ¾ in. (10.2 x 17.1 cm)
Private collection

After he expatriated to Italy in 1866, Vedder embarked on countless leisurely sketching trips with his own countrymen—notably William Graham (1832–1911), Thomas Hiram Hotchkiss (1833–69; figs. 134–135), and Charles Caryl Coleman (1840–1928)—and Italians, such as the Roman Nino Costa (1826–1903). Although Vedder was best known in America for his visionary allegorical and mythical paintings—pensive prophets, wild-eyed Medusas, a man questioning the Great Sphinx at Giza—he preferred painting in nature, despite the difficulties it sometimes posed:

> The landscapes required long walks over hill and dale, and when perspiring, getting at once to work so as not to lose some effect, perhaps catching it and a cold at the same time. Sometimes working surrounded by a grinning crowd and hearing their unflattering comments, or perchance attended by a solitary boy with a bad cold in his head, munching an apple; this last is a fearful thing and is as dangerous to one's peace of mind as sheep are to foreground plants. Then coaxing people to pose,—and on returning, tired out, washing your brushes, as I have frequently done, when virtuous. After your outing, on returning to town, the mere handling and care of thirty-six pictures, seeing to the framing, and so forth, is hard work.[64]

In Vedder's oil sketches from the 1860s and 1870s, such as *Bridge at Narni* (fig. 138) and *View from Via Sistina 72, Rome* (fig. 136), the Macchiaioli effect is somewhat modulated, but the artist's fascination with light and atmosphere is undiminished.

Many of Vedder's peers shared his empirical attitude toward outdoor painting. Graham's overcast view of dormant trees in *By the Tiber near Rome, Winter* (fig. 139) bears an uncanny resemblance to Vedder's *Winter Landscape* (fig. 140) in subject and *coup de l'oeil* approach, in which artists present a view as though it were seen at a glance rather than selectively framed. Like Vedder's *Baths of Caracalla, Santa Balbina, and the Tomb of Caius Cestius from the Palatine Hill* (fig. 142), Samuel Colman's (1832–1920) *View of the Campagna from the Baths of Caracalla* (fig. 141) evinces a fascination with the changing effects of light as it plays across the moldering brickwork and colored stucco of the city and grows

*Below*
Fig. 148. PANORAMIC VIEW
OF THE AQUEDUCTS, ca. 1884
John Severinus Conway (1852–1925)
Oil on canvas
9 x 25 in. (22.9 x 63.5 cm)
Private collection

hazy as the scene encompasses the ruin-littered Campagna. Colman's *Nymphaeum and Tor de' Schiavi, Villa Gordiani* (fig. 144) and Henry Augustus Loop's (1831–95) *The Claudian Aqueducts at Twilight* (fig. 143) function primarily as color studies, displaying an evident delight with recently invented cadmium pigments that freed artists to paint vividly hued sunsets. Compared to Loop's earlier oil sketch of *Old Gate at Nemi* (fig. 145), we can detect a new level of confidence as an open-airist.

During his second sojourn in Italy (the first was in 1851–52), George Inness (1825–94) made dozens of open-air oil sketches, such as *Roman Campagna (Ponte Nomentano)* (fig. 146). While the glimpse of sky indicates an ostensibly cloudy day, on closer inspection of the landscape we discern that the cloud cover is actually very high, permitting sunlight to filter through and silver the distant plateau, while the soft rise in the middle ground is thrown into shade. An unseen cumulus cloud makes its presence known by the dark swath it casts in the far right background. It is a deceptively complex painting by a master technician. One anecdote, related by Maitland Armstrong, demonstrates the strength of Inness' visual acuity:

> I was one day sketching one of these ruins, a small temple or tomb, the stucco a delicious yellowish tint, with a bright spot of white in the centre of the apse-like top. An almond-tree in bloom hung over it, and beyond was a jumble of delicate flowers and a touch of tender blue sky. I was busily absorbed when I looked up and saw George Inness and T. Buchanan Read. They had just finished lunching together and were in good spirits. Inness remarked, "Your high light in the arch is not bright enough." So, handing him my palette and brush, I said, "Do it yourself then," and without taking off his kid gloves he took the brush, mixed up some Naples-yellow and white, steadied himself and gave one dab just in the right spot. I sold that sketch later for a hundred dollars, but whether it was because of Inness's master touch I never knew.[65]

Beginning in 1883 John Severinus Conway (1852–1925), better remembered as a sculptor, made Rome his home for the next twenty years. He produced hundreds of oil sketches during that time, including the unfinished *View of Aqueducts at Twilight* (fig. 147). It was, he noted, "done mostly from memory," but he aborted the effort out of frustration, writing along the bottom of the panel how he had failed to capture the colors and mood without his model before him:

> Effect of aqueducts was lighter against sky. Mountains more roseate; blue and sunlit parts more blended. All detail much massed but sharp. Other color and effect misty, just a plain, simple russet, very, very sober and strange. Pristine effects, scenery varied only in the blue tone.

In Conway's *Panoramic View of the Aqueducts* (fig. 148), shapes are abstracted in deference to the painter's interest in color: cerulean-stained mountains and ocherous dry grasses bisected by the stunning whiteness of a ground marble-topped

*Above*
Fig. 149. PASTORAL SCENE ON THE CAMPAGNA, not dated
Samuel Lancaster Gerry (1813–1891)
Charcoal with touches of white chalk on gray wove paper
15 ¾ x 22 in. (40 x 55.8 cm)
Private collection

*Opposite*
Fig. 150. RUINS IN ITALY, ca. 1870–77
William Louis Sonntag (1822–1900)
Oil on canvas
9 ½ x 11 ½ in. (24.1 x 29.2 cm)
Private collection

road. The ancient Roman aqueducts that had previously attracted American painters—Thomas Cole, George L. Brown, Sanford R. Gifford, Worthington Whittredge, and Henry A. Loop, to name but a few—for their classical associations as much as for their visual impact are here relegated to secondary status. It is a haunting image that suggests the oil sketch's shift away from its traditional role as an accurate transcription of the natural world and heralds an increasing interest in the artist's unique vision of it.

# Notes

1. Of the more influential catalogues devoted to the topic see Rudolf Wittkower, intro., *Masters of the Loaded Brush: Oil Sketches from Rubens to Tiepolo* (New York: Columbia University, 1967); Theodore E. Stebbins Jr., *Close Observation: Selected Oil Sketches by Frederic E. Church* (Washington, DC: Smithsonian Institution Press, 1978); Lawrence Gowing, *Painting from Nature: The Tradition of Open-Air Oil Sketching from the Seventeenth to the Nineteenth Centuries* (London: Arts Council of Great Britain, 1980); Peter Galassi, *Corot in Italy: Open-Air Painting and the Classical Landscape Tradition* (New Haven: Yale University Press, 1991); Philip Conisbee, Sarah Faunce, and Jeremy Strick, *In the Light of Italy: Corot and Early Open-Air Painting* (Washington, DC: National Gallery of Art, 1996); Christopher Riopelle and Xavier Bray, *A Brush with Nature: The Gere Collection of Landscape Oil Sketches* (London: National Gallery Publications, 1999).

2. Peter Galassi, *Before Photography: Painting and the Invention of Photography* (New York: The Museum of Modern Art, 1981), 24.

3. Philip Conisbee, Sarah Faunce, and Yukitaka Kohari, *Plein-air painting in Europe 1780–1850* (Sydney: Art Gallery of New South Wales, 2004), 11.

4. Irene Weir, *Robert W. Weir, Artist* (New York: House of Field-Doubleday, Inc., 1947), 9.

5. Ibid., 21.

6. Dumont and Hosack, *Catalogue of Valuable Oil Paintings, Studies and Sketches, &c., by John G. Chapman, Artist, To Be Sold at Auction, At 62 White Street, Wednesday, April 19th, 1848* (New York: Dumont and Hosack, 1848). This catalogue tantalizingly lists thirty-eight oil sketches done in Italy, most of which are captioned "painted on the spot."

7. John Gadsby Chapman, *The American Drawing-Book: A Manual for the Amateur* (New York: J. S. Redfield, 1858), 236–37.

8. Ibid.

9. Rembrandt Peale, *Notes on Italy* (Philadelphia: Carey and Lea, 1831), 187. For an example of Peale's work from Tivoli, see Theodore E. Stebbins Jr., et al, *The Lure of Italy: American Artists and the Italian Experience 1760–1914* (New York: Harry N. Abrams, Inc., 1992), 159.

10. Ibid., 187–88.

11. Samuel F. B. Morse, Italian Journal, April 6, 1830, Samuel F. B. Morse Papers, Library of Congress, Washington, DC.

12. Ibid., May 5, 1830.

13. Chapman, *Drawing-Book*, 237–38.

14. James Edward Freeman, *Gatherings from an Artist's Portfolio* (New York: D. Appleton and Company, 1877), 266.

15. Morse, Italian Journal, June 16, 1830.

16. Ibid., June 17, 1830.

17. Thomas Cole as quoted in William Dunlap, *History of the Rise and Progress of the Arts of Design in the United States*, 2 vols. (New York: George P. Scott and Co., 1834), 2:364.

18. Louis Legrand Noble, *The Life and Works of Thomas Cole*, ed. Elliot S. Vesell (Cambridge, Massachusetts: The Belknap Press of Harvard University Press, 1964), 109.

19. John Cranch, Italian Journal, August 30, 1831, John Cranch Papers, 1831–1892, Archives of American Art, Smithsonian Institution.

20. Ibid., September 3, 1831.

21. Thomas Cole, draft manuscript of "Visit to Volterra," August 24-ca. September 4, 1831, Thomas Cole Papers, 1821–1863, owned by New York State Library, Albany, New York.

22. Noble, *Thomas Cole*, 114.

23. Ibid., 115.

24. Ibid., 111–12.

25. Ibid.

26. Thomas Cole to Robert Gilmor Jr., undated draft of a letter after May 10, 1835, as quoted in *Annual II: Studies on Thomas Cole, an American Romanticist* (Baltimore: Baltimore Museum of Art, 1967), 79.

27. Chapman, *Drawing-Book*, 236.

28. John I. H. Baur, ed., *The Autobiography of Worthington Whittredge 1820–1910* (New York: Arno Press, 1969), 55.

29. For other examples of Cole's open-air oil sketches see Eleanor Jones Harvey, *The Painted Sketch: American Impressions from Nature, 1830–1880* (New York: Harry N. Abrams, 1998), 114–25.

30. Marcel Roethlisberger, *Claude Lorrain: The Paintings*, 2 vols. (New Haven and London: Yale University Press, 1961), 1:47–48.

31. Ibid., 1:48–49.

32. Thomas Cole to Robert Gilmor Jr., *Annual II*, 79.

33. For an image of this work, see Roethlisberger, *Claude Lorrain*, 2:fig. 169.

34. This work is reproduced in Elwood C. Parry III, *The Art of Thomas Cole: Ambition and Imagination* (Newark: University of Delaware Press, 1988), 122. The finished version, *The Protestant Cemetery in Rome*, 1834, is housed at The New York State Office of Parks, Recreation and Historic Preservation, Bureau of Historic Sites, Olana State Historical Site, Taconic Region.

35. Henry Willard French, *Art and Artists in Connecticut* (Boston: Lee and Shepard, Publishers, 1879), 100.

36. John F. Kensett to Sarah D. Kellogg, October 1, 1846, John F. Kensett Papers, 1832–1872, New York State Library, Albany, New York.

37. Ibid.

38. George William Curtis, "Editor's Easy Chair," *Harper's New Monthly Magazine* 46, no. 274 (March 1873): 611–12.

39. Thomas B. Ashton to James Cameron, February 4, 1848, James and Emma Cameron Papers, Mills College, F. W. Olin Library, Special Collections.

40. Jasper F. Cropsey to Thomas Cole, March 16, 1848, Thomas Cole Papers. Sadly, Cole never read this letter due to his untimely death on February 11, 1848.

41. Margaret Fuller, *"These Sad but Glorious Days": Dispatches from Europe, 1846–1850*, ed. Larry J. Reynolds and Susan Belasco Smith (New Haven and London: Yale University Press, 1991), 200.

42. William Cullen Bryant, *Letters of a Traveller* (New York: D. Appleton and Co., 1850), 238.

43. Baur, *Whittredge*, 38. For a drawing of this bed by Gifford, see Ila Weiss, *Poetic Landscapes: The Art and Experience of Sanford R. Gifford* (Newark: University of Delaware Press, 1987), 195. Thomas Buchanan Read (1822–72).

44. Baur, *Whittredge*, 36.

45. For an image of this work, see Anthony F. Janson, *Worthington Whittredge* (Cambridge: University of Cambridge, 1989), 68.

46. Gifford to his father, February 5, 1857, Sanford Robinson Gifford Papers, typescript, Archives of American Art, Smithsonian Institution.

47. *Catalogue Part II of The Gifford Collection, Comprising Balance of the Valuable Paintings, Works of and Belonging to the Estate of the Late Sanford R. Gifford, N. A.* (New York: Thomas E. Kirby and Co. Auctioneers, April 29, 1881), no. 87.

48. G. W. Sheldon, *American Painters* (New York: D. Appleton and Company, 1879), 16.

49. Sanford Robinson Gifford Papers, European Letters, March 25, 1857, typescript.

50. F., "Foreign Correspondence, Items, Etc.," *Crayon* 4, no. 7 (July 1857): 219.

51. David Maitland Armstrong, *Day before Yesterday: Reminiscences of a Varied Life* (New York: Charles Scribner's Sons, 1920), 167.

52. Gifford, European Letters, May 4, 1857.

53. Peter Frederick Rothermel to Joseph Patterson, October 7, 1857, The Winterthur Library, Joseph Downs Collection of Manuscripts and Printed Ephemera, No. 57x18.98.

54. E., "Foreign Correspondence, Items, etc.," *Crayon* 5, no. 6 (June 1858): 170.

55. "Studios of American Artists," *Home Journal* (March 22, 1856): 1.

56. "Sketchings. Domestic Art Gossip," *Crayon* 6, no. 12 (December 1859): 379–80.

57. Henry T. Tuckerman, *Artist-Life: or, Sketches of American Painters* (New York: D. Appleton and Company, 1847), 155.

58. Chapman, *Drawing-Book*, 3.

59. William Cullen Bryant II and Thomas G. Voss, eds., *The Letters of William Cullen Bryant*, 6 vols. (New York: Fordham University Press, 1984), 4:44.

60. "Art, Music, and the Drama," *Putnam's Magazine* 3, no. 13 (January 1869): 110. William Wetmore Story (1819–95), Randolph Rogers (1825–92), Emma Stebbins (1815–82), Harriet Hosmer (1830–1908), Margaret Foley (1820–77), Joseph Mozier (1812–70), Luther Terry (1813–1900), John Rollin Tilton (1828–88), Hamilton Gibbs Wild (1827–84), Frederic Edwin Church (1826–1900), George Henry Yewell (1830–1923), Launt Thompson (1833–94), Henry Wadsworth Longfellow (1807–82), and Cyrus West Field (1819–92).

61. Gifford, European Letters, January 8, 1869.

62. Ibid., November 2, 1868.

63. Elihu Vedder, *The Digressions of "V": Written for His Own Fun and That of His Friends* (Boston: Houghton Mifflin Co., 1910), 139.

64. Ibid.

65. Armstrong, *Day before Yesterday*, 198.

# Selected Bibliography

**Archival Sources**

Brown, George Loring. Account Book, 1851–1859. Owned by Museum of Fine Arts, Boston, William Morris Hunt Library; microfilmed by the Archives of American Art, Smithsonian Institution.

Henry Kirke Brown Papers, 1836–1893. Manuscript Division, Library of Congress; microfilmed by the Archives of American Art, Smithsonian Institution.

Thomas Cole Papers, 1821–1863. Owned by New York State Library, Albany, New York; microfilmed by the Archives of American Art, Smithsonian Institution.

John Cranch Papers, 1831–1892. Archives of American Art, Smithsonian Institution.

Sanford Robinson Gifford Papers, 1840s–1900. Archives of American Art, Smithsonian Institution.

Huntington Family Papers, 1792–1901. Owned by Channing M. Huntington II; microfilmed by the Archives of American Art, Smithsonian Institution.

John F. Kensett Papers, 1832–1872. New York State Library, Albany, New York; microfilmed by the Archives of American Art, Smithsonian Institution.

Samuel Finley Breese Morse Papers, Manuscript Division, Library of Congress, Washington, DC.

**Articles and Books**

Anderson, Nancy K. and Linda S. Ferber. *Albert Bierstadt: Art and Enterprise.* New York: Hudson Hills Press, 1990.

Armstrong, David Maitland. *Day before Yesterday: Reminiscences of a Varied Life.* Edited by Margaret Armstrong. New York: Charles Scribner's Sons, 1920.

Basham, Ben L. *Conrad Wise Chapman: Artist and Soldier of the Confederacy.* Kent, Ohio: Kent State University Press, 1998.

Baur, John I. H. *The Autobiography of Worthington Whittredge, 1820–1910.* New York: Arno Press, 1969.

Bellinger, Katrin. *Out into Nature: The Dawn of Plein-Air Painting in Germany, 1820–1850.* London: Colnaghi, 2003.

Berman, Avis. "Sketch Club of American Artists at Rome." *Archives of American Art Journal* 40, nos. 1-2 (2000): 2–3.

Bignamini, Ilaria and Martin Postle. *The Artist's Model: Its Role in British Art from Lely to Etty.* Nottingham: Nottingham University Art Gallery, 1991.

Brown, David Blayney. *Oil Sketches from Nature: Turner and His Contemporaries.* London: Tate Gallery, 1991.

C. "Fine Arts. English Academy at Rome." *London Literary Gazette* no. 320 (March 8, 1823): 155.

———. "Fine Arts. Anglo-Roman School." *London Literary Gazette* no. 329 (May 10, 1823): 298.

Cavina, Anna Ottani, et al. *Paysages d'Italie: Les peintres de plein air (1780–1830).* Milan: Electa, 2001.

Chapman, John Gadsby. *The American Drawing-Book: A Manual for the Amateur.* New York: J. S. Redfield, 1858.

Cheney, Ednah. *Memoirs of Seth W. Cheney, Artist.* Boston: Lee and Shepard, 1881.

Conisbee, Philip, Sarah Faunce, and Jeremy Strick. *In the Light of Italy: Corot and Early Open-Air Painting.* Washington, DC: National Gallery of Art, 1996.

Conisbee, Philip, Sarah Faunce, and Yukitaka Kohari. *Plein-air painting in Europe, 1780–1850.* Sydney: Art Gallery of New South Wales, 2004.

Crane, Susan Underwood. "Edward Sheffield Bartholomew." *Connecticut Quarterly* 2 (January-December 1896): 203–14.

Di Castro, Francesca. *Via Margutta: Cinquecento anni di storia e d'arte.* Rome: Edizioni Kappa, 2006.

Driscoll, John Paul and John K. Howat. *John Frederick Kensett: An American Master.* New York: Worcester Art Museum with W. W. Norton and Company, 1985.

Dumont and Hosack. *Catalogue of Valuable Oil Paintings, Studies and Sketches, &c., by John G. Chapman, Artist.* New York: Dumont and Hosack, 1848.

Dunlap, William. *History of the Rise and Progress of the Arts of Design in the United States.* 2 vols. New York: George P. Scott and Company, 1834.

Dupont, Christine A. *Modèles italiens et traditions nationales: Les artistes belges en Italie (1830–1914).* 2 vols. Brussels and Rome: Institut Historique Belge de Rome, 2005.

Eldredge, Charles. *The Arcadian Landscape: Nineteenth-Century American Painters in Italy.* Lawrence, Kansas: University of Kansas Museum of Art, 1972.

Farley, Joseph Pearson. *Three Rivers: The James, the Potomac, the Hudson. A Retrospect of Peace and War.* New York and Washington: The Neale Publishing Company, 1910.

Fink, Lois Marie and Joshua C. Taylor. *Academy: The Academic Tradition in American Art.* Washington, DC: National Collection of Fine Arts, Smithsonian Institution, 1975.

Freeman, James Edward. *Gatherings from an Artist's Portfolio.* New York: D. Appleton and Company, 1877.

——. *Gatherings from an Artist's Portfolio in Rome.* Boston: Roberts Brothers, 1883.

French, H. W. *Art and Artists in Connecticut.* Boston: Lee and Shepard, Publishers, 1879.

Galassi, Peter. *Before Photography: Painting and the Invention of Photography.* New York: Museum of Modern Art, 1981.

——. *Corot in Italy: Open-Air Painting and the Classical Landscape Tradition.* New Haven: Yale University Press, 1991.

Gardiner, William. *Sights in Italy.* London: Longman, Brown, Green, and Longmans, 1847.

Gowing, Lawrence. *Painting from Nature: The Tradition of Open-Air Oil Sketching from the Seventeenth to the Nineteenth Centuries.* London: Arts Council of Great Britain, 1980.

Greenwood, Grace. *Haps and Mishaps of a Tour in Europe.* Boston: Ticknor, Reed, and Fields, 1854.

Griswold, William M., et al. *The Thaw Collection: Master Drawings and Oil Sketches, Acquisitions since 1994.* New York: The Pierpont Morgan Library, 2002.

Harvey, Eleanor Jones. *The Painted Sketch: American Impressions from Nature, 1830–1880.* Dallas: Dallas Museum of Art in association with Harry N. Abrams, 1998.

Jandolo, Augusto. *Studi e Modelli di Via Margutta (1870–1950).* Milan: Casa Editrice Ceschina, 1953.

"A Journey from Westminster Abbey to St. Peter's." *Bentley's Miscellany* 34 (1853): 506–18.

Katlan, Alexander. "The American Artist's Tools and Materials for On-Site Oil Sketching." *Journal of the American Institute for Conservation* 38, no. 1 (1999): 21–32.

Keyes, Donald D., et al. *George Cooke, 1793–1849.* Athens, Georgia: Georgia Museum of Art, 1991.

Leland, Henry P. *Americans in Rome.* New York: Charles T. Evans, 1863.

MacKinnon, James. *Paintings and Sketches, 1780–1860.* Bradford, England: Polestar (Fine Arts) Printers, 2002.

——. *Aspects of Landscape, 1760–1880.* London: Watmoughs Printers, 1996.

Mammucari, Renato. *Ottocento romano: Le indimenticabili immagini dei pittori, italiani e stranieri, che immortalarono luoghi e personaggi della Città Eterna.* Rome: Newton Compton Editori, 2007. Reprint of 1993 edition.

McGuigan Jr., John F. and Mary K. McGuigan. *James E. Freeman 1808–1884: An American Painter in Italy.* Utica, New York: Munson-Williams-Proctor Arts Institute, 2009.

*National Academy of Design Exhibition Record 1826–1860.* 2 vols. New York: New-York Historical Society, 1943.

Noble, Louis Legrand. *The Life and Work of Thomas Cole.* Edited by Elliot S. Vesell. Cambridge, Massachusetts: The Belknap Press of Harvard University Press, 1964.

Olson, Roberta J. M., ed. *Ottocento: Romanticism and Revolution in 19th-Century Italian Painting.* New York: American Federation of Arts and Centro Di della Edifimi, 1992.

"Origin of the English Academy. [From a copy of the Circular, printed at Rome, with which we have been favoured]." *London Literary Gazette* no. 322 (March 22, 1823): 188.

Parry III, Elwood C. *The Art of Thomas Cole: Ambition and Imagination.* Newark: University of Delaware Press, 1988.

Peale, Rembrandt. *Notes on Italy, by Rembrandt Peale. Written During a Tour in the Years 1829 and 1830.* Philadelphia: Carey and Lea, 1831.

[Rippingille, Edward Villiers]. "An Evening's Gossip with a Painter. Palette and Chatworthy in Conversation." *Artist and Amateur's Magazine* (February 1844): 344–59.

Quick, Michael. *George Inness: A Catalogue Raisonné.* 2 vols. New Brunswick, New Jersey, and London: Rutgers University Press, 2007.

Richardson, Edgar P. and Otto Wittmann Jr. *Travelers in Arcadia: American Artists in Italy, 1830–1875.* Detroit: Detroit Institute of Arts, 1951.

Riopelle, Christopher and Xavier Bray. *A Brush with Nature: The Gere Collection of Landscape Oil Sketches.* London: National Gallery Publications, 1999.

Sharp, William. *The Life and Letters of Joseph Severn.* London: Sampson Low, Marston, and Company, 1892.

Simon Dickinson, Inc. *Rome and the Campagna: Auguste Jean-Baptiste Vinchon and Other French Artists.* New York: Simon Dickinson, Inc., 1999.

Soria, Regina. *Elihu Vedder: American Visionary Artist in Rome (1836–1923).* Rutherford, New Jersey: Fairleigh Dickinson University Press, 1970.

——. *Dictionary of Nineteenth-Century American Artists in Italy.* Rutherford, New Jersey: Fairleigh Dickinson University Press, 1980.

Stebbins Jr., Theodore E. *Close Observation: Selected Oil Sketches by Frederic E. Church.* Washington, DC: Smithsonian Institution Press, 1978.

——. *The Lure of Italy: American Artists and the Italian Experience, 1760–1914.* Boston: Museum of Fine Arts, Boston, in association with Harry N. Abrams, 1992.

Stuart, Henri L. *William H. Powell's Historical Picture of "The Discovery of the Mississippi by De Soto, A.D. 1541."* New York: Baker, Godwin, and Company, 1853.

Tuckerman, Henry T. *Artist-Life: or, Sketches of American Painters.* New York: D. Appleton and Company, 1847.

——. *Book of the Artists: American Artist Life.* New York: G. P. Putnam and Son, 1867.

Vance, William L. *America's Rome.* 2 vols. New Haven and London: Yale University Press, 1989.

Waller, Susan. *The Invention of the Model: Artists and Models in Paris, 1830–1870.* Aldershot, England: Ashgate Publishing Limited, 2006.

Weir, Irene. *Robert W. Weir, Artist.* New York: House of Field-Doubleday, 1947.

Weiss, Ila. *Poetic Landscape: The Art and Experience of Sanford R. Gifford.* Newark: University of Delaware Press, 1987.

Wittkower, Rudolf, intro. *Masters of the Loaded Brush: Oil Sketches from Rubens to Tiepolo.* New York: Columbia University, 1967.

# Lenders to the exhibition

America's Rome:
Artists in the Eternal City, 1800–1900

Addison Gallery of American Art

Albany Institute of History & Art

Brooklyn Museum

Butler Institute of American Art

Cincinnati Art Museum

Columbus Museum of Art

Corcoran Gallery of Art

Currier Gallery of Art

Davis Museum and Cultural Center,
Wellesley College

Detroit Institute of Arts

The Frances Lehman Loeb Art Center,
Vassar College Art Gallery

Howard Gotlieb Archival Research Center,
Boston University

The Metropolitan Museum of Art

Montclair Art Museum

Museum of Fine Arts, Houston

New Britain Museum of American Art

New-York Historical Society

The Newark Museum

Newington-Cropsey Foundation

North Carolina Museum of Arts

Private Collection

Private Collection, Texas

Spanierman Gallery

The Toledo Museum of Art, Ohio